Salvation

The Covenant Journey

Todd D. Bennett

Shema Yisrael Publications

Salvation – The Covenant Journey

First printing 2015

ISBN: 9780985000455
Library of Congress Control Number: 2015911863

Printed in the United States of America.

Please visit our website for other titles:
www.shemayisrael.net

For information write:
Shema Yisrael Publications
123 Court Street
Herkimer, New York 13350

For information regarding publicity for author interviews call
(866) 866-2211

Salvation

The Covenant Journey

*"¹⁵⁵ Salvation is far from the wicked,
for they do not seek Your statutes . . .
¹⁶⁶ LORD (יהוה), I hope for Your salvation,
and I do Your Commandments."*
Psalms 119:155, 166

Table of Contents

Salvation

Christianity is a religion with a distinct focus on salvation. In fact, in order to be called a Christian you must be "saved." Exactly what it means to be saved is a question that we will examine in this book. Generally, Christians believe that it involves a present decision that results in an immediate guarantee of going to heaven in the future, after you die.

It is important to understand that the notion of salvation has transformed over the centuries from a very present and tangible concept to a more distant and abstract idea.

When the Messiah made His triumphal entry into Jerusalem prior to His crucifixion, the people cried out "Hosanna"[1] which means: "save now". They were not talking about going to Heaven. They were hoping that He was going to save them from the oppression of the Romans and establish the restored Kingdom of Yisrael there and then. Their concept of salvation was a very real and present expectation in the physical realm.

Of course, during His ministry the Messiah dealt with the debate concerning the resurrection, which is the ultimate goal of salvation – deliverance from death. He definitively answered that question through His own resurrection. He later ascended into the clouds, but the plan was not to leave this planet for good. The Messiah said He would return in the clouds, but first He would prepare a place for His Bride.

So beyond the death, resurrection and ascension of the

---

[1] The actual word in Hebrew and Aramaic is "Hoshea-na" (הושע-נא). It is actually the name of the prophet Hosea (Hoshea) and the Patriarch who had his name changed from Hoshea to Joshua (Yahushua). This will become very significant as this discussion continues.

Messiah, there is also a future expectation that will involve a return of the Messiah to this earth, a resurrection of the dead, the restoration of the Kingdom of Yisrael and ultimately the renewed Jerusalem descending upon the earth. Thereafter, the Messiah will rule over a restored planet and the Kingdom with His Bride. Within this future framework there will also be a judgment of all who lived upon the planet.

So where does the Christian understanding of salvation fit into this plan? That is a question that we will be exploring. According to popular Christian doctrine a person "converts" to the Christian religion and becomes a Christian when they are saved by praying a certain prayer, often called "The Sinner's Prayer".

Once they say the prayer they are deemed "saved", which means they will go to heaven when they die. There are many variations of the prayer, but they all typically list the following steps:

1) Confess that you are a sinner
2) Repent from your sins
3) Accept Jesus Christ as your personal savior

Sometimes a prayer is not required at all. The conversion process may involve an altar call or, in larger evangelical settings, it may simply involve raising your hand "while every eye is closed" so as not to make the person feel uncomfortable or embarrassed by expressing their desire to be saved.

Imagine that! We wouldn't want someone to be uncomfortable when they choose to be saved. After all, in most of Christianity, conversion is considered to be an internal decision when you make Jesus Christ your *personal* savior.

So salvation, at least in modern Christianity, has become a fairly quick and easy process. With the accompanying doctrine of "once saved always saved"[2] salvation essentially becomes a box that is checked on a "to do" list at some point in a person's life. Once that prayer is said and that box is checked, the person can then move on with their life knowing that their future is "eternally secure".

It sounds like a great deal. Imagine an eternal future in Heaven in return for just a few seconds or minutes of your time. Who wouldn't take that deal? This is the ideal religious solution for an impatient society obsessed with convenience. Sadly, rather than being grounded in truth, this process and belief has its roots in our self-centered, fast-food, drive thru mentality.

If you think that all you have to do to be saved is answer an altar call, say a prayer, or raise your hand at a church service, then you are sadly mistaken. You have been deceived, you've been taught a lie and now you believe it.

Nowhere in the Bible do we ever read about Moses, a Prophet or the Messiah detailing this process of salvation. Rather, the Scriptures describe a continuous Covenant that ran from Noah to Abraham, then through Yisrael[3] until it was ultimately renewed by the Messiah Himself.[4]

There are some critical flaws with the Christian

---

[2] Not all Christians believe this doctrine, but it has become very pervasive in modern Christianity. It essentially teaches that once you have made that decision you are saved and you can never lose that salvation. As we proceed with this discussion the fallacy of the argument should become clear.

[3] Yisrael is the proper transliteration from the Hebrew language for the Covenant Assembly described in the Scriptures, which includes all of the Tribes descending from the Man Jacob, whose name was changed to Yisrael. It also includes all those who chose to follow the Mighty One of Yisrael and enter into Covenant with Him. The identity of these people is often confused with the single Tribe of Judah or the Kingdom of Judah commonly called "The Jews" or "The Jewish People". The true identity of Yisrael is described in the Walk in the Light Series book entitled *The Redeemed*.

[4] For a detailed discussion of the Covenant process described in the Scriptures see the Walk in the Light series book entitled *Covenants*.

understanding of salvation, the first being that it begins and ends with a decision. Instead of salvation being a future event, Christianity treats it like an immediate present event accomplished and completed at "the moment of decision." After that decision, a person considers that they have been "saved" and presently are "saved". They do not tend to see it as something that will occur at a later time.

It is important to put the notion of salvation into proper context. There is such a thing as an immediate life or death salvation, but that is not the same as the salvation of our souls. If you see me drowning and throw me a lifeline then you saved my life. When the Yisraelites, and the mixed multitude departing from Egypt during the Exodus, were delivered through the waters of the Red Sea they were saved from Pharaoh's army.[5]

Indeed, the Scriptures provide numerous examples of people being delivered from judgment, death, destruction, hunger, thirst etc. These are all examples of salvation. In contrast, we are not saved from the effects of death until we actually experience physical death. At that point we hope to be saved from the punishment of sin, which leads to eternal separation from the Creator.

---

[5] The people were told to *"behold and see the salvation of the LORD."* Exodus 14:13. There is a great mystery in the Hebrew as the word for "salvation" (יְשׁוּעַת) is affixed to a special and mysterious word known as the Aleph Taw (אֶת), which often represents the Messiah. The "aleph" (א) is the first letter in the Hebrew alphabet and the "taw" (ת) is the last letter in the Hebrew alphabet. It represents and contains all of "the words" in the Hebrew language and it is "the word" that is found in the texts from the beginning (Genesis 1:1) referred to in the Book of John (John 1:1) and specifically revealed to represent the Messiah (Revelation 1:8, 1:11 and 21:5). In the modern Hebrew text of Exodus 14:13 we see "the salvation" revealed as: "אֶת-יְשׁוּעַת". This hints to a future and greater salvation for Yisrael through the Messiah. For a further discussion of this mysterious reference to the Messiah that can only be witnessed in the Hebrew language see the Walk in the Light series book entitled *The Messiah*. Also, the Hebrew text in Exodus 14:13 does not refer to "the LORD", but uses the actual Name of the Creator. See Footnote 7.

It is our hope that when our physical bodies die, we receive resurrected bodies and be permitted to be with the Creator for all of eternity. Understandably, Christians desire an immediate resolution to this eternal life or death issue, but it involves much more than simply a prayer.

Upon making that "decision" or saying a prayer, a new Christian convert may be given a New Testament or a Gospel of John and told to attend a local church. Sadly, they are rarely, if ever, directed onto the Covenant path walked and taught by the Messiah. As a result, most Christians utterly fail to understand the Covenant that actually defines the relationship between the Creator and His people, and it is only through that relationship that a person will find salvation.

The Creator in the Scriptures, Who enters into a Covenant relationship with His people, is described as Elohim, not God.[6] He has a Hebrew title – Elohim, and He also has a Hebrew Name.[7] This Creator, Who identifies Himself with the Hebrew language and through the Hebrew culture also revealed how mankind could repair their broken relationship with Him through the ancient Covenant process.

So the decision to "convert" or say a sinner's prayer is often deficient or flawed because the one saying the prayer rarely knows that they must enter into Covenant in order to be saved. While they recognize the need to be saved from the penalty of their sins, most of the time they simply confess that they are a sinner.

This is really not an earth-shattering event since everyone is a sinner. All they are doing is stating the obvious.

---

[6] It is important to understand that the Creator first described Himself in the Hebrew language. The word Elohim is a title and the Creator also has a Name revealed in Hebrew.

[7] The Name of the Creator is depicted as four Hebrew characters – "yud" ('), "hey" (ה), "vav" (ו), "hey" (ה) known as the Tetragrammaton (יהוה). This subject is detailed in the Walk in the Light series book entitled *Names*. It is also detailed further in this book.

It is a good start though, because confession is an important step that leads to repentance, and this leads to the real question which is: How do we know we are sinners and what are we prepared to do about that fact?

2

Repentance

Rarely is sin defined in Christianity, despite the fact that confessing you are a sinner is an integral part of the conversion process. The Scriptures are very clear regarding the definition of sin. According to 1 John 3:4 - "*Whoever commits sin also commits lawlessness, and sin is lawlessness*".

So, we know from the Scriptures that the definition of "sin" is "lawlessness", but what exactly is lawlessness? In the Greek manuscripts the word for "lawlessness" is "anomia" (ἀνομία).[8] It means: "without the Torah" or "in violation of the Torah".

The word Torah (תורה) is actually a Hebrew word rarely heard in Christianity, despite the fact that it is at the heart of the Covenant made between Elohim and His people. In the simplest sense it means "instructions", although most English translations of the Bible choose to translate it as "the Law".[9]

The Torah contains the instructions given by the Creator to show mankind how to live righteous lives so that we can dwell in His presence. The instructions include the Commandments that we read in what is commonly referred

---

[8] The word for sin in Hebrew is "chata" (חטא) and it means: "to miss the mark" or "to go astray". There is a righteous way established by the Creator and it is set forth in His instructions, known as the "Torah" (תורה).

[9] The Torah is a very misunderstood word because it is often translated into English as "the Law." Most Christians have been conditioned to perceive "the Law" as oppressive and bad when the Torah is actually the exact opposite. The Hebrew word "Torah" derives from two Hebrew roots that involve pointing in the right direction and then moving in that direction. The Torah is often referred to as the five Books of Moses or the Torah of Moses. Sometimes the word Torah is used interchangeably with Moses as it can be seen in Acts 15:21.

to as the Old Testament.[10] I do not like using that phrase because while those texts may be old, the Covenant that they describe is critical for us to understand today. In fact, it is in the Torah that we find the definition of sin - the act of violating or the omitting to follow the Commandments of Elohim.

Therefore, before a person can truly confess that they are a sinner, they need to understand the Commandments and identify specifically why they are a sinner. Once you identify what sins you have committed, only then are you in a position to confess those sins and repent.

Now, repentance is a critical act, but it is also often misunderstood by Christians. Many equate it to being remorseful or feeling sorry for your sins. Repentance is much more than a feeling – it involves action. The act of repentance is often called "teshuvah" (תשובה) in Hebrew and it means "to turn."

The idea is that, if you are not following the Commandments, you repent by turning back to Elohim and His Commandments. A person who "backslides" is one who has turned away from the Commandments. We have examples of what backsliding involves by looking at the past conduct of Yisrael.[11]

---

[10] The use of the term "Old Testament" to describe the Torah, the Prophets and the Writings is not appropriate. It gives the distinct impression that the contents are somehow old, outdated, irrelevant and replaced by the "New Testament". Nothing could be further from the truth. While those texts describe events in the past, so do the texts in the "New Testament". The texts referred to as the "Old Testament" are foundational to our faith and are just as relevant today as they were at the time of their writing. In fact, they contain many patterns and prophecies that await a future fulfillment.

[11] It must be made clear that we are not referring to the Modern State of Israel that was founded in 1948, in large part, by Jewish settlers motivated by Zionism. Rather, we are referring to Yisrael, the set apart assembly of people who follow the commandments of Elohim and rely of the shed blood of the Messiah to make themselves clean. This Yisrael is a nation of priests who follow the Great High Priest, Yahushua the Messiah. The

The people of Yisrael were supposed to be set apart as a nation of priests who would be an example to the rest of the world.[12] They were to obey the Commandments and receive the blessings associated with living in Covenant with their Creator. Through their obedience, they would draw all the nations to Elohim, and teach them the ways of Elohim found in the Torah.

Sadly, they failed to fulfill their mandate through obedience. Elohim warned them that if they did not teach the nations through their obedience, then the nations would still be taught through Yisrael's disobedience.[13]

Many look at Yisrael as a failed experiment that the Creator scrapped because of their sin. Nothing could be further from the truth. Yisrael was and continues to be the Covenant people of Elohim. They were promised blessings for obedience and curses for disobedience. Even after they were punished, Elohim promised that their Covenant relationship would be restored.

Here is a description of the repentance required from Yisrael.

"[40] But if they confess their iniquity and the iniquity of their fathers, with their unfaithfulness in which they were unfaithful to Me, and that they also have walked contrary to Me, [41] and that I also have walked contrary to them and have brought them into the land of their enemies; if their uncircumcised hearts are humbled, and they accept their guilt - [42] then I will remember My Covenant with Jacob,

---

Covenant people are called a "qahal" (קהל) in Hebrew, also known as an "assembly" or "congregation". The Hebrew pronunciation of the Covenant Assembly is "Yisrael". We will use that spelling because it helps distinguish the Covenant Assembly described in the Scriptures from the Modern State of Israel. These two different entities are not to be confused. This subject is discussed in greater detail in the Walk in the Light series book entitled *The Redeemed*.

[12] *"And you shall be to Me a kingdom of priests and a holy nation."* Exodus 19:6

[13] See Deuteronomy 28 and 29:24-28

and My Covenant with Isaac and My Covenant with Abraham I will remember; I will remember the Land. [43] The Land also shall be left empty by them, and will enjoy its Sabbaths while it lies desolate without them; they will accept their guilt, because they despised My judgments and because their soul abhorred My statutes. [44] Yet for all that, when they are in the land of their enemies, I will not cast them away, nor shall I abhor them, to utterly destroy them and break My Covenant with them; for I am the LORD (YHWH) their Elohim. [45] But for their sake I will remember the Covenant of their ancestors, whom I brought out of the land of Egypt in the sight of the nations, that I might be their Elohim: I am the LORD (YHWH)." Leviticus 26:40-45

This is the repentance required for Yisrael to be restored to the Covenant. Anyone can join in with Yisrael when they enter into a Covenant relationship with Elohim and that Covenant is found in the Torah.[14]

When we refer to Yisrael we are not talking about the Jewish State known as the modern State of Israel in the Middle East. That nation was founded as a secular state, primarily focused on the notion of Zionism, not the Torah.

---

[14] It is important to understand that when Yisrael was delivered out of Egypt they included the descendants of the man named Yisrael as well as *"a mixed multitude of people"* (Exodus 12:38). This mixed multitude were likely circumcised and participated in the Passover by being covered by the blood of the Lamb of Elohim. They joined into Covenant with Elohim through this meal and were grafted into Yisrael. Part of the Covenant involved eating the Lamb. This is why Yahushua said: *"[47] Most assuredly, I say to you, he who believes in Me has everlasting life . . . [54] Whoever eats My flesh and drinks My blood has eternal life, and I will raise him up at the last day."* John 6:47,54. We must partake of the Messiah's Passover and enter into the Covenant renewed by Messiah's broken body and shed blood. As a result, the Torah applied to all who were in the set apart Assembly of Yisrael. *"One Torah shall be for the native-born and for the stranger who dwells among you."* Exodus 12:49. See also Leviticus 24:22, Numbers 9:14, 15:15, 15:29 and Isaiah 56.

When we refer to the Covenant Assembly of Yisrael, we are talking about the people around the world who are in a covenant relationship with Elohim demonstrated by their obedience to the Commandments of Elohim found in the Torah.[15]

This is a greatly misunderstood and confused subject, but it is imperative to understand these labels and terms in order to properly interpret the Scriptures, and particularly the prophecies contained within the texts. For instance, you cannot simply apply prophetic passages concerning the divided and exiled Kingdom of Yisrael to the Modern State of Israel.

The Kingdom of Yisrael was punished in the past because of her sins. She was divided into two separate kingdoms known as the house of Yisrael and the house of Judah. The house of Yisrael was first conquered and exiled by the Assyrians. The house of Judah was later conquered and exiled by the Babylonians. Both were given unique punishments, but were promised that if they repented and returned to YHWH they would be reunited and restored.

The Messiah came according to the Torah and the Prophets to atone for her sins and pave the way for her restoration. That restoration of the divided Kingdom has still not been completed. Through that restoration, all the nations may join in the Covenant as the Children of Yisrael are re-gathered and delivered by the Hand of the Great Shepherd.

If you believe in the teachings and the atoning work of the Messiah, then you want to be joined to the Covenant Assembly of Yisrael. This is the only set apart assembly of people in Covenant with YHWH.[16]

---

[15] The subject of the identity of the Covenant people Yisrael is discussed in the Walk in the Light series book entitled *The Redeemed*.

[16] Christianity has developed the notion of the Christian "Church" as a separate group of people that are joined to Elohim. This tradition that developed over time is based upon anti-Semitism and the friction that occurred between early followers of Messiah and the Pharisaic sect of

When Yisrael violated the Covenant she was considered "backslidden". Here is a description of backslidden Yisrael: "*Because My people have forgotten Me, they have burned incense to worthless idols. And they have caused themselves to stumble in their ways, from the ancient paths . . .*" Jeremiah 18:15

The passage describes Yisrael as having stepped off of the righteous path that leads to life. That path is the ancient Covenant path described in the Torah. Instead of walking that path, Yisrael chose to whore after false gods and worship them. She had "broken the yoke" and "burst the restraints" which guided the righteous way.[17] She had chosen to disobey and go astray down the road to destruction. It is a problem that has plagued mankind since the Garden of Eden.[18]

Sadly, those who say the sinner's prayer rarely are explained that they are supposed to turn back to the Commandments. Instead they are told to acknowledge that

---

Yisraelites that opposed them. The notion of "the church" being separate from or replacing Yisrael is not accurate or Scriptural. The Messiah did not come to start a new religion. Instead He came to seek out the "*lost sheep of the house of Yisrael*" (Matthew 15:24). He was a shepherd looking for His scattered sheep in order to bring them back into the fold through the renewed Covenant instituted at the Passover meal, (known as the Last Supper), and perfected through His subsequent death and resurrection.

[17] See Jeremiah 5:4-5 and Jeremiah 6:16. The way of the Master is where we find blessing and rest for our souls. In order to stay on this ancient and righteous path we must be willing to take on His yoke and be steered by His restraints (bonds). This is the purpose of the Commandments – to guide us to and keep us on the righteous path that leads to blessing.

[18] Eden is a Hebrew word that means "paradise". Paradise is the dwelling place of the Creator and only the redeemed, who guard and protect the Commandments, can dwell there. This is why the man and the woman were expelled. They violated the Commandments. Since then, man has been outside of paradise and we need to "turn" (repent) to the path that leads back to Eden. That path is revealed through the Torah, which contains the righteous instructions of the Creator. The atonement required to enter through that door was represented by the blood of the Lamb at Passover.

they are sinners. This leads to them viewing repentance as a sort of apology - like saying they are sorry for sinning. That is not true repentance, because they typically are not told what they are turning away from or what they are turning toward. They typically have no idea that they are joining into a Covenant, and they rarely are shown the terms of the Covenant contained within the Torah.

The Christian conversion process is flawed because repentance clearly involves a turning away from sin, which is defined as violating the Commandments. Therefore, an essential part of repenting involves turning away from sin and returning to the righteous instructions found in the Commandments. Only when one turns and walks according to the Commandments have they truly repented. This is not simply a decision - it is a way of life.

Of course, this is what the Messiah was demonstrating as He walked and taught the people. He was showing them how to live according to the Commandments as Elohim intended. He was preparing them and directing them onto the righteous path and away from the traditions of men. This is something missed by many who fail to understand the true purpose of the Messiah as savior.

3

The Savior

The process of accepting Jesus as your personal savior is problematic because the Jesus that is taught in Christianity is not the same Yahushua[19] Who was born into the Tribe of Judah, was the very Torah in the flesh, lived and taught the Commandments, Renewed the Covenant with the House of Yisrael and the House of Judah, died as the Lamb of Elohim on Passover, rose from the grave and then sent The Spirit on the Appointed Time of Shavuot.

You see, the Messiah[20] was a Yisraelite with the Hebrew name Yahushua. He instructed and empowered His followers to obey the Commandments, while the Jesus of Christianity supposedly did the exact opposite.

---

[19] The Messiah was a Yisraelite from the Tribe of Judah (Yahudah). He had the same Hebrew Name as the Patriarch commonly called Joshua. The Hebrew Name is spelled with either 5 letters (יהושע) or 6 letters (יהושוע) and is pronounced Yahu-shua. It contains the short form of the Name of the Father (Yahu) and the Hebrew root word for salvation (yasha), which is where we get the name Hosea, the original name of Joshua son of Nun (Numbers 13:16). The Name of the Messiah points to His emphasis on salvation as described by the Messenger on the Book of Matthew. *"And she will bring forth a Son, and you shall call His name Yahushua, for He will save His people from their sins."* Matthew 1:21. Sadly, you will not find the correct Hebrew Name Yahushua in most Bibles because they are modern translations of Greek texts, in which, certain names were Hellenized and changed from their original. It is quite certain that the true Name of the Messiah was the same as that of Joshua, more accurately transliterated from Hebrew as Yahushua. For a more detailed discussion of the Name of the Messiah see the Walk in the Light series book entitled *Names*.

[20] The English word "Messiah" comes from the Hebrew word "moshiach" which literally means "anointed". In the Scriptures it could refer to a King or a Priest. Both positions involved being anointed with oil. The Messiah is the One anticipated to merge those two positions together as the Melchizedek – the Righteous King.

His proper Hebrew Name actually means "Yah saves" or "Yah is salvation". "Yah" represents the short form of the Name of the Father.[21] This is why the Messiah is also referred to as the Savior. His purpose is to save the Covenant people. In fact, when Joseph was told what to name Him, this description was given as the meaning of His Name – *"he shall save His people from their sins".*[22]

"His people" are those in Covenant and their sins are defined by and through the Covenant. The terms of the Covenant are found in the Torah. Therefore, the entire life and ministry of Yahushua was a fulfillment of the patterns contained within the Torah.[23]

So the very focus of the salvation provided by the Messiah involves the Torah, but according to most Christians, Jesus did away with the Law by abolishing the Torah. They actually believe that Jesus lived a perfect life according to the Torah, and then destroyed the very definition of His perfection - as if the Torah is a bad thing. Indeed, the entire concept is an oxymoron, because this would involve the Torah in the flesh destroying Himself.

The true Savior would have never done such a thing since He was the very embodiment of the Word of Elohim – the Torah in the Flesh (John 1:14). He walked, taught and lived the Torah as an example for us. He taught the *truth*, shined as a *light,* and showed us the *way* to *life*. Of course these were all descriptions of the Torah.

"For the Commandment is a lamp, and the Torah a light;

---

[21] As a result, Yahushua literally came in His Father's Name. See John 5:43. The Name of the Father will be discussed further in this book.

[22] See Matthew 1:21. Again, in an English Bible you will read the name Jesus, but that is simply a translation tradition. The real Name is Yahushua and it unequivocally reveals the purpose of the Messiah, which is to save the people of Yah from their sins. By sending His Son, Yah will save His people from their sins.

[23] For a more detailed discussion of the patterns and prophecies fulfilled by the Messiah see the Walk in the Light series book entitled *The Messiah.*

reproofs of instruction are <u>the way of life</u>."
Proverbs 6:23

*"Your righteousness is an everlasting righteousness,
and <u>Your Torah is truth</u>."*
Psalm 119:142

Sadly, through language variations and the traditions of men, Christianity has developed a fictional christ named Jesus who is very different from the actual Hebrew Messiah named Yahushua.[24] This is a difficult statement for many to accept due to the strongly held traditions that they have inherited.

Almost every English speaking Christian came into the faith calling on "the Name of the LORD" and "Jesus". Neither of these references are Scripturally sound, but most people are reticent to correct their understanding and speech. They think that by doing so, they will somehow be abandoning their faith. The English title and name are deeply ingrained within most Christians and very near and dear to their hearts. As a result, it is hard to accept that some of the doctrines we all have been taught and believed throughout our lives are grounded in tradition and even lies.

The power of tradition is undeniable. Christians regularly participate in pagan derived holidays such as Christmas and Easter. Most fail to understand that these holidays originate from Babylonian sun worship rituals and were erroneously adopted by the Christian religion. Sadly, even when confronted with the truth most refuse to give them up.[25] When people develop pleasant memories and

---

[24] A presentation of the actual life, teaching and purpose of the Messiah within a proper historical and Scriptural context is provided in the Walk in the Light series book entitled *The Messiah*.

[25] For a more detailed discussion of the pagan traditions that have infiltrated the Christian religion see the Walk in the Light series book entitled *Pagan Holidays*.

- 16 -

emotional attachments with certain traditions they often would rather continue in a lie than give up their tradition to follow the truth.

Of course we should expect much deception if we believe the prophets. The prophet Jeremiah foretold of a time when *"the Gentiles shall come to You from the ends of the earth and say, 'Surely our fathers have inherited lies, worthlessness and unprofitable things.'"* Jeremiah 16:19.

Those familiar with the Scriptures know that there is a deceiver who seeks the worship of men.[26] Through lies and traditions, the serpent seeks to divert the worship of mankind away from the One True Elohim to himself. He has been doing this ever since the Garden, when he called Elohim a liar. Through seduction and deceit he led the woman and the man away from the Commandments. He continues those same tactics to this day and has most of the world under a spell through various diversions and religions that steer mankind away from the truth. Somehow, Christians believe that they are immune from deception, but the Scriptures tell otherwise.[27]

Christians have indeed inherited many lies from their fathers as prophesied by Jeremiah. One of those inherited lies involves the name of the Messiah. It is important to understand that the name Jesus never existed in ancient times, nor was it ever spoken in the Hebrew, Aramaic or Greek languages that were prevalent at the time of Messiah's arrival over 2,000 years ago. The Messiah was not named Jesus nor was anyone named Jesus at that time. The name simply did not exist.

It was not until the English language developed that the name of Jesus was spoken, because there is no letter J in

---

[26] See Isaiah 14: 12-15. Also, the words spoken to "the prince of Tyre" and "the King of Tyre" in Ezekiel 28 are thought by many to also apply to satan.

[27] See 1 Timothy 4:1-3. Also see the warnings in Matthew 24:24 and Mark 13:22.

the languages spoken in ancient times.[28] In fact, the letter J is a fairly recent addition to linguistics, coming into existence only about 400 years ago.[29]

This is not simply about the spelling or pronunciation of a name though. In the Hebrew culture names are very important and describe the essence of a person. The Hebrew name Yahushua is the same name as the one we call Joshua in English. We are supposed to make the connection between the Messiah and that Patriarch who brought the Covenant Assembly of Yisrael into the Promised Land. So if you were to call the Messiah by an English name, at the very least, you should call Him Joshua - which means "Yah saves His people".[30]

---

[28] The English language developed between the 14th century and the 17th century. Most agree that the letter J did not come into existence until the 1600's. Therefore, the name "Jesus" has only been in existence for about 400 years. Prior to that time the Greek name "Iesus" prevailed and it is apparent that the name "Iesus" was used to replace the true Hebrew Name Yahushua. This is a historically provable fact. There is no debate on this at all. When someone insists on calling the Messiah Jesus, it is because they have chosen a tradition over truth. I don't care how long they have called on this name, how much they revere this name or how deeply they think they were saved by this name - it was not the name of the Messiah described in the Scriptures. While they may have expressed faith in the One described in the Scriptures, it is critical that they correct their traditions according to the truth.

[29] The letter "J" derived from the letter "I" and originally carried the "Y" sound. It was not until the early 1600's that the letter was pronounced with the "jay" sound. So to properly transliterate both the Names of the Messiah and the Patriarch, it should pronounced Yahushua.

[30] Of course, the English Name Joshua is also incorrect because it contains a "J" but the English transliteration better connects to the original Hebrew Name that it is supposed to represent. The name Jesus is not connected to the Hebrew Name Yahushua at all in either a translated or transliterated sense. In any event, when we transition from one language to another we are supposed to transliterate names so that they sound the same from language to language. Sadly, people who have been brought up with the tradition of calling the Messiah by a fictitious name cling to this tradition rather than adopt the truth. I believe that the Messiah appreciates when we use His real Name and certainly knowing someone's

- 18 -

The Name defines the very purpose and function of the work of the Messiah. While Joshua, the servant of Moses, eventually led Yisrael into the Promised Land, the Messiah fulfills that same pattern. As Yisrael crossed the Jordan from the Land of Moab into the Land of Canaan they were corporately "baptized" in the Jordan. They were then circumcised and proceeded to conquer and inhabit the Promised Covenant Land.

Through the death and resurrection of the Messiah we can now be baptized in the Spirit and have our hearts circumcised. As a result, we can enter into the Promised Land, which represents a return to the Garden and the Kingdom of Elohim.

The Messiah came to fulfill these patterns and in order to place His teachings and ministry into context it is important to understand this connection. The name Jesus, on the other hand, derives from unknown or possibly pagan sun worship origins.[31] It was not and is not the name of the Messiah.[32] The name Iesus was inserted into Greek texts in

---

name is an important part of having a close relationship with them. This is not to say that people who learned the traditional name of Jesus cannot know Him but, once we learn the truth, we become accountable for what we do with that truth. Again, when we use the Hebrew Name, we connect it with the work of the Hebrew Messiah Who lived, walked and taught the Torah. In Christianity, most believers use the Hellenized Greek name Jesus in reference to their Christ, whom they present as abolishing the Torah. These are two diametrically opposed individuals. The subject of the Name of the Messiah is discussed further in the Walk in the Light series book entitled *Names*.

[31] Again, the English name "Jesus" derives from the Greek name "Iesus". It is not etymological linked to the Hebrew Name Yahushua, which clearly contains the Name of the Father. In John 5:43, the Messiah unequivocally stated "*I have come in My Father's Name . . .*" On one hand, that involves coming in the authority vested in Him by His Father but, on the other hand, it literally involves the fact that His Name includes the Name of the Father. The Name of the Father is discussed further in this book.

[32] Again, this is an extremely important issue for people to recognize if they have been calling upon the name of Jesus and worshipping Jesus

place of the true Name.[33] That Greek name was later translated as Jesus in the English language.

Christianity also uses the title "Christ" which was a Greek title used to describe the Greek gods. Of course, these Greek gods all derived from sun worship that can be traced back to ancient Babylon.

So a Greek name and title, both rooted in Babylonian sun worship, have been adopted by Christians to refer to the Hebrew Messiah. This mistake is more than simply a linguistic technicality; it has far-reaching theological implications. As it turns out, the Christian "Christ", represented through Christian tradition, is in many ways diametrically opposed to the true Messiah described in the Scriptures.

We have the clear words and teachings of Yahushua in the texts that are often ignored or twisted to fit the lawless paradigm created by Christianity. As a result, the Jesus of Christianity has morphed into a sort of anti-christ or anti-messiah.[34] The Christian religion has attempted to replace the

---

their entire lives. Thankfully, Elohim knows the thoughts and intents of the heart of men. He knows when we are calling upon Him and He is patient with us when we operate out of ignorance. Once He reveals the error of our way, we are obligated to "repent" and correct our mistakes.

[33] The name Iesus is connected with the name of a healing god and a child of Zeus, the Greek king of the gods. It is likely that converts to Christianity, many of whom came out of sun worship, replaced the name to identify Yahushua as the Son of God. This type of thing clearly occurred with the New Testament texts. For example, the name of the prophet Elijah is rendered as Helios in the Greek texts. Of course Helios is the name of the Greek god of the sun. It makes perfect sense that the same would be done with the "Son of God".

[34] This seems impossible for most Christians to comprehend, but this is critical to understand. Again, Yahushua specifically warned of such an event. *"For false christs and false prophets will rise and show great signs and wonders to deceive, if possible, even the elect."* Matthew 24:24. See also Mark 13:22. The Hebrew Messiah was the living Torah. He did not come to abolish the Torah, a thing commonly attributed to the Christian Jesus.

Torah teaching Yahushua with a Law abolishing Jesus.[35]

Of course this should be no surprise because the one described as "antichrist", or rather "anti-messiah" in First and Second John is not simply opposed to the Messiah. He seeks to replace the Messiah and receive the worship, the throne and the authority that belongs to Yahushua.

Paul referred to this individual as "the lawless one" (2 Thessalonians 2:8) and the hallmark of this lawless one will be his opposition to the Torah.

So, if Christians believe that their Christ abolished the Torah, then they worship an "anti-christ" - more accurately called an "anti-messiah". These are hard words and this is a hard truth. Many have difficulty accepting them, but there is no gentle way of presenting these facts. The enemy seeks to deceive the elect through false christs and false prophets. This was clearly foretold by Yahushua.

"For false christs (messiahs) and false prophets will rise and show
signs and wonders to deceive, if possible, even the elect."
Matthew 24:2, Mark 13:22

What better way to deceive the elect than to hijack the identity of the One he opposes and hates. As a result of this deception, most Christians believe that the Commandments are no longer applicable to the people of Elohim. This is why they have no Scriptural definition of sin and this is why they fail to point converts to the Covenant path.

They erroneously equate "obedience" with "legalism", as if obeying the Commandments was something repulsive and to be avoided. This is only a problem if you think that

---

[35] This is often a difficult concept for Christians to grasp. Of course, a paradigm shift is never easy, but this one is critical. You must understand that the Jesus espoused by Christianity does not accurately represent the Messiah Yahushua. You must determine who you follow and that is demonstrated by how you live.

you can earn your salvation through obedience. You cannot work your way into the Kingdom, but your works will definitely determine your place in the Kingdom.[36]

The only way to get into the Kingdom is to pass through the door covered by the blood of the Lamb. This is why Passover is the first Appointed Time in the yearly cycle of special times that we are commanded to observe.[37] It reveals that the way into the Covenant journey is by the shed blood of the Lamb of Elohim. The key is that you must walk through the door into the Covenant within which the blood was shed. Obedience is simply our loving response to the free gift of atonement provided to us through that shed blood.[38]

Yahushua came according to the Covenant promises to prepare a people who will truly love and serve Elohim - a people who will be His Bride. That is why His true disciples repent and are then baptized in His Name. By doing so, they acknowledge His authority to forgive sins.

---

[36] "Whoever therefore breaks (relaxes) one of the least of these Commandments, and teaches men so, shall be called least in the kingdom of heaven; but whoever does and teaches them, he shall be called great in the kingdom of heaven." Matthew 5:19.

[37] For a detailed discussion of the timing and meaning of the annual Appointed Times, see the Walk in the Light series book entitled Appointed Times.

[38] Yahushua specifically said: "If you love Me, keep My Commandments" John 14:15.

4

Baptism

The first recorded sermon of any of the disciples of Yahushua is recorded in the Book of Acts when Peter declared on the Day of Pentecost (Shavuot): *"Repent, and let every one of you be baptized in the Name of Yahushua Messiah for the remission of sins; and you shall receive the gift of the Holy Spirit."* Acts 2:38[39]

Notice that Peter first instructed people to repent. This was the very same message spoken by John the Baptist and it was also the message proclaimed by the Messiah.

"[1] In those days John the Baptist came preaching in the wilderness of Judea, [2] and saying, 'Repent, for the kingdom of heaven is at hand!'"
Matthew 3:1-2

"From that time Yahushua began to preach and to say, 'Repent, for the kingdom of heaven is at hand.'"
Matthew 4:17

This was a message spoken to Yisraelites who had strayed from the Commandments, and in it they were instructed to turn back to the Commandments.

Peter was specifically speaking to Yisraelites who had gathered at the Temple in Jerusalem to celebrate the festival known as Weeks, or Shavuot in Hebrew.[40] These people

---

[39] You will notice that this passage reads differently than the typical English translation that uses the wrong name and title. In the remaining portion of this book translation errors will often be corrected in order to provide clarity and consistency for the reader.

[40] The word "Pentecost" is a Greek word that literally means: "fiftieth." This is because the Feast of Shavuot occurs on the fiftieth day after the first offering of barley that takes place during the Feast of Unleavened Bread. The actual count to Shavuot involves counting seven weeks, which

were already obeying the Torah and would likely have immersed themselves as they were bringing their firstfruit offerings to present in the Temple.

Thus Peter was not instituting some new ritual called "baptism". The Yisraelites were very familiar with the immersion process as they would regularly immerse themselves in a "mikvah".[41] It was a ritual cleansing process that all would undergo before they could meet with Elohim in His House. When they emerged from the waters they would declare themselves to be "born again" after being washed clean. It was a pattern and understanding that was practiced long before Yahushua came to fulfill those patterns.

In fact, in one of his letters Peter likened baptism to a fulfillment of the pattern of Noah and the flood. While the sins of the planet were washed away through the flood waters, Noah and the occupants of the Ark were baptized and passed safely through them. They were saved and delivered from judgment, and were allowed to enter into the renewed creation and covenant with the Creator. Likewise, those who are baptized in the Name of Yahushua will pass through a future judgment and enter into a renewed creation through the renewed Covenant.[42]

---

is 49 days. A day is then added which leads to the 50th day - Shavuot. For a more detailed discussion of Shavuot and the other Appointed Times see the Walk in the Light book entitled *Appointed Times*. Understanding these times is critical for those interested in their prophetic fulfillment described in the Scriptures.

[41] A mikvah is a place where people would immerse or baptize themselves. The ideal place to immerse is in a river or body of "living water". Sometimes that was not readily available so special pools were constructed for immersion.

[42] See 1 Peter 3:18-22. It is significant to note that Peter emphasizes the eight souls in the Ark. The number eight is an important number as it points to new beginnings through the Covenant. While an individuals Covenant journey begins on the eighth day of their life when they are circumcised, the annual cycle of the Appointed Times actually ends on "the eighth day", often referred to as Shemini Atzeret. For further information on the number eight as it relates to the Covenant and the

It is important to stress that Peter was specifically telling the people to immerse in the Name of Yahushua. He did not tell them to immerse in the Name of Jesus, because the name of Jesus did not even exist at that time. Again, Jesus is an English word that only came into existence when the English language was developing about 500 years ago.

We know from Peter that getting the Name right is important. In fact, it is necessary for our salvation. He specifically stated: *"Nor is there salvation in any other, for there is no other Name under heaven given among men by which we must be saved."* Acts 4:12.

Now, if you read an English translation, a previous verse (Acts 4:10) will tell you that the name is Jesus Christ, but the actual Name is Yahushua and His title is Messiah - Yahushua the Messiah.

Thus salvation comes through the Name Yahushua because the Name literally means: "Yah saves". It acknowledges that only the Son of Yah, who receives His authority from the Father, can save us from the penalty associated with our sins. We are instructed to be immersed in that Name, because it is through the Word made flesh that we are cleansed. Only then will we be able to approach Him and have a relationship with Him. By this immersion we acknowledge that Yahushua has authority to forgive our sins.

This would have made perfect sense to a Yisraelite who was accustomed to the rehearsals conducted at the Temple.[43] They understood that each Yisraelite needed atonement as individuals and Yisrael needed atonement as a nation. This was rehearsed each year on Yom Kippur – The

---

Appointed Times see the Walk in the Light series books entitled *Covenants* and *Appointed Times*.
[43] The use of the name Jesus is one reason why many Jews refuse to accept the Christian Christ as their Messiah. They know that is is a false name and could not be the Name of the Messiah.

Day of Atonement.[44]

You see, the shedding of the blood of animals was always a pattern that pointed to a necessary atonement through the shedding of blood. *"And according to the Torah almost all things are purified with blood, and without shedding of blood there is no remission."* Hebrews 9:22.[45]

The baptism is symbolic of the cleansing they receive by the blood of the Messiah. That is why it is important to be baptized in the Name and authority of Yahushua. Yahushua is the Messiah, and that is what gives Him the authority. It is by His blood that you receive the cleansing. Interestingly, the baptism is also the same ritual cleansing that the bride undergoes before her wedding. She must present herself without spot or blemish to her groom.

This is why the first recorded miracle of the Messiah involved turning water into wine at a wedding.[46] At the Last Supper, when He renewed the Covenant, He said that the wine represented His blood. The union of the husband and

---

[44] The Day of Atonement is a very special Appointed Time. It occurs on Day 10 of the 7th Scriptural month. The atonement procedure is described in Leviticus 16. Every 50 years this day would also mark the beginning of the Year of Jubilee. (see Leviticus 25:9). Sadly, most of the world is unfamiliar with this day because they live under a pagan calendar derived from the Roman Empire. The Scriptural Calendar and the Appointed Times are discussed in the Walk in the Light series books entitled *Appointed Times* and *Pagan Holidays*.

[45] The English translation of this passage refers to "The Law" but the actual meaning is "The Torah." The Torah includes the righteous instructions of the Creator.

[46] The miracle at Cana is recorded in the text of John at Chapter 2. It is no coincidence that Yahushua performed this miracle at a wedding. He actually used water from stone vessels designated for the waters of purification. They specifically held water that was used for ritual cleansing. It is likely that these stone vessels were empty, because the bride had just used them for her purification prior to the wedding. It was the water in those vessels that symbolized cleansing. That water of purification was then turned into wine. We know that at the Last Supper, when the Messiah instituted the Passover meal He declared that the wine represented His blood. So His blood would result in cleansing His Bride.

the wife, while they consummate their covenant relationship, involves the shedding blood. Indeed, the blood stained sheet from the marriage bed was the token, or sign, that the marriage covenant had been consummated.

Here is what Paul provided on the subject: *"25 Husbands, love your wives, just as Messiah also loved the assembly and gave Himself for her, 26 that He might sanctify and cleanse her with the washing of water by the word, 27 that He might present her to Himself a glorious assembly, not having spot or wrinkle or any such thing, but that she should be holy and without blemish."* Ephesians 5:25-27

The "word" in this passage is "rhema" (ῥῆμα) in the Greek. It means "utterance" and it refers to the spoken word. This would include the Commandments of Elohim, and the Messiah who was the Word in flesh. Yahushua taught the Torah and He was the embodiment of the Torah in a vessel of flesh.

To be "sanctified" is to be set apart. Some refer to it as "holy". So the act of being washed by the Word involves being obedient to the Word so that you conduct yourself in a righteous manner. Through your obedience you stay clean.

Again, this does not mean that you earn your salvation. It only means that you recognize the need to be cleansed and once you receive the cleansing you need to remain set apart from sin. The Bride of the Messiah is actually washed by the Torah and the blood of the Messiah. This was confirmed by Peter.

"22 Since you have purified your souls in obeying the truth through the Spirit in sincere love of the brethren, love one another fervently with a pure heart, 23 having been born again, not of corruptible seed but incorruptible, through the word of Elohim which lives and abides forever."
1 Peter 1:22-23

None of these are new formulas exclusively developed

for the Christian religion. There were no Christians when these texts were written, nor was there even a Christian religion in existence at that time. That would not occur until centuries later when the Roman Empire created the Christian religion.[47]

Remember that Yisrael was the Bride of Elohim who had been punished and was awaiting restoration. This is the context of Yahushua's ministry. He came to restore the Bride, Yisrael, by providing the needed cleansing and atonement through a Renewed Covenant.

So if you believe in the Messiah then you need to join the proper Covenant and identify with His true Bride. Then, after you receive cleansing from the blood of Yahushua through faith, you need to stay clean. You stop sinning because you repented from your lawlessness and turned to walk in the path of obedience.

Sadly many people accept the free gift provided by the shed blood of the Lamb of Elohim, but instead of entering through the door of the Covenant, they reject the Covenant, refuse to enter through the door and, rather than staying clean, they continue to sin and wallow in the filth of lawlessness.

Many do this mistakenly believing that they are "under grace". They fail to understand that grace was the offer of forgiveness provided through the blood of the Lamb.

---

[47] This may be one of the most misunderstood events in history. While growing up in Christianity, I was always taught that Christianity was a religion started by Jesus and centuries later the Roman Emperor Constantine was miraculously converted to Christianity after which he made it the official state religion of the Roman Empire. To the contrary, the evidence is overwhelming that the Messiah did not come to start a new religion, but rather, to restore the Kingdom of Yisrael. Constantine remained a shrewd and ruthless politician and sun worshipper to his death. Christianity was actually a religion created by the Roman Empire that specifically rejected the Commandments and mixed the belief in the Messiah with popular sun worship traditions. This is a well-documented historical fact for those interested in researching the truth.

It does not mean that they have a license to sin. This is one of the greatest lies perpetrated through Christianity, and it mainly stems from a failure to understand the Covenant.

5

The Covenant

One thing is certain, Yahushua did not come to die for individuals who are not interested in joining the Assembly of Yisrael through the renewed Covenant. While His blood is available for all to be cleansed, that atonement must occur through the very Covenant for which His blood was shed.

Therefore, you do not ask Jesus into your heart, you ask Yahushua to circumcise your heart. A circumcision event involves shedding blood, which is integral to the formation of any covenant. The circumcision of the heart occurs when one enters into the Renewed Covenant through the Messiah. The circumcision occurs on the very organ that pumps the blood and maintains life in the body.[48]

The Renewed Covenant prophesied by Jeremiah involves putting the Torah in our minds and writing it on our hearts so that we can be called the people of Elohim.

"[31] Behold, the days are coming, says YHWH, when I will make a renewed covenant with the house of Yisrael and with the house of Judah [32] not according to the Covenant that I made with their fathers in the day that I took them by the hand to lead them out of the land of Egypt, My Covenant which they broke, though I was a husband to them, says YHWH. [33] But this is the Covenant that I will make with the house of Yisrael after those days, says YHWH:

---

[48] The blood represents our life. The Scriptures clearly indicate that the life of the flesh is in the blood. *"For the life of the flesh is in the blood, and I have given it to you upon the altar to make atonement for your souls; for it is the blood that makes atonement for the soul."* Leviticus 17:11. Since the heart is the central organ for maintaining and distributing that life force, the heart is the central part of the Covenant that offers atonement and everlasting life. As a side note, it has been discovered that the heart is much more than simply a pump. It is a gland that emits hormones and it actually emits a powerful energy field.

I will put My Torah in their minds, and write it on their hearts;
and I will be their Elohim, and they shall be My people."
Jeremiah 31:31-33

You may have noticed the Name of Elohim provided
as YHWH in the passage above. This is not what you will
find in any English translation of the Bible. Through
traditions and translations the Name has been hidden and
replaced with the title "The LORD". Here is the Name in
both the modern Hebrew יהוה and in the ancient Hebrew as
ᕁᕁᕁᕁ.[49]

Hebrew reads from right to left and displaying the
Name as YHWH represents the Hebrew consonants in the
English language from left to right. The letter "Y" represents
the Hebrew letter "yud" (ᕁ). The letter "H" represents the
Hebrew letter "hey" (ᕁ). The letter "W" represents the
Hebrew letter "vav" (ᕁ) also known as "waw". The last
letter "H", again, represents the Hebrew letter "hey" (ᕁ).

The Name is pronounced "ya-hoo-wah".[50] The
emphasis is on "Yah" which is the poetic short form of the
Name of the Father, as already discussed being in the Name
of the Son. The shortened Name can actually be seen in some
passages of English translations of the Bible such as Isaiah
12:2.

---

[49] The ancient Hebrew Script is the most authentic form of the Hebrew
language. It includes pictographs that actually represent the meaning of
the individual characters.
[50] There are some who believe that the Name is unspeakable, but that is
completely inconsistent with the Scriptures where we read about people
repeatedly calling upon the Name and worshipping the Name. Not only
is there disagreement about whether or not the Name should be spoken,
but also there is disagreement over how one should pronounce the Name.
A popular pronunciation is "Yahweh", but this does not seem to properly
account for the way we pronounce other names that include the Name of
YHWH. The pronunciation of the Name is discussed further in the
Walk in the Light series book entitled *Names*.

"Behold, God is my salvation, I will trust and not be afraid; for YAH, the LORD, is my strength and song; He also has become my salvation."

Isaiah 12:2 NKJV

The passage would be more accurately translated into English as follows:

"Behold, Elohim is my salvation, I will trust and not be afraid; for YAH, YHWH, is my strength and song; He also has become my salvation (yashua)."

This text is of particular importance to this book because it states that: *"Yah, YHWH has become my salvation (yashua)."* So we actually see short form Name of Messiah (Yashua) hidden in this text as the salvation of YHWH.[51] He became our salvation through His Son, Who came in the flesh and in the Father's Name (John 5:43).

Again, it is important to know the Name of YHWH, because this is the Name by which we are saved. Remember that the Name of the Messiah is Yahushua. It means: "Yah saves" or "Yah is salvation."

Now back to the prophecy found in Jeremiah 31. If you read the passage in a typical English translation, it probably describes a "new" covenant, but the Hebrew word used is "chadash" (חדש), which is the same root as the one used to describe a "new" moon – "chodesh" (חדש).

We all know that the moon goes through a monthly cycle, beginning at the first sliver and waxing to a full moon, then waning to darkness.[52] When we see the first sliver again

---

[51] As previously discussed, the Name of the Messiah contains the Name of YHWH (Yah) and the root of the word "salvation" (yasha and Hoshea). So the Name of the Messiah is couched in this verse. Yashua is actually a short form of the Name Yahushua.
[52] This is actually how a month is determined by the Creator. The sun and the moon act as hands on the clock for planet Earth. Sadly, much of

we call it a "new moon", but we know it is the same moon that we saw only a few days previously. It is not a brand new moon, but rather a renewed moon.[53]

The same holds true with the Covenant. It is not a brand new covenant that the Prophet was referring to, but rather a renewed covenant. This is critical to recognize. If you believe that Elohim established a brand new covenant and started a brand new religion you will utterly fail to understand His plan to draw in the nations to Him through a restored house of Yisrael at the end of days.

This is what the prophets foretold: that the Torah will literally be at the heart of the future restoration. Only then the Torah that had been written on stone and animal hide scrolls will be written in the minds and on the hearts of people in Covenant with Elohim. It will become alive within us.

This process is exactly what Ezekiel was referring to when he prophesied to the house of Yisrael. "*I will give you a new heart and put a new spirit within you; I will take the heart of stone out of your flesh and give you a heart of flesh.*" Ezekiel 36:26. Here again, the word for "new" in Hebrew is "chadash" (חדש), which is the same root used to describe the "renewed" moon and the "renewed" Covenant. Ezekiel is referring to what will happen when the Covenant is renewed as described

---

the world reckons time according to the pagan Roman sun calendar that exhalts Roman deities and emperors through the names of the days and months. This varies from the way the Creator reckons time and that is why much of the world fails to understand prophetic timelines. The subject of the Creator's Calendar is discussed in detail in the Walk in the Light series book entitled *Appointed Times*.

[53] Astronomy has developed a different standard for the new moon at the conjunction when the moon is in darkness. This differs from the historical understanding of the new moon when it once again becomes visible after being in darkness. It is the first light of the renewed lunar cycle and has great spiritual significance. Thus the new moon at the first sliver is actually a renewal of the moon through its monthly cycle – not a new moon.

by Jeremiah.

This is why the Word became flesh. Yahushua, as the Word in the flesh, had the Torah in His mind and heart. His vessel of flesh contained the Spirit as prophesied by Isaiah.[54] He walked out the Commandments perfectly and showed us the way to do it. He showed us that true obedience begins with the heart and is centered in love – love for YHWH and love for our neighbor.[55] He then died so we can be cleansed. Afterward, He sent the Spirit to write the Torah on our minds and hearts so that we can be set apart. If you want to be part of the Bride you must understand this truth.

Now consider the renewed Covenant provided through Jeremiah. Notice that there is no mention of a lawless Christian Church. Rather, the Covenant is being renewed with the original Bride – the house of Yisrael and the house of Judah. Recall from history that, after the death of King Solomon, Yisrael was divided into two kingdoms: 1) the house of Yisrael, and 2) the house of Judah. The Scriptures, particularly the texts of Kings, Chronicles and the Prophets, show how Elohim dealt with each house separately.

Both houses sinned and were separately exiled and uniquely punished. The house of Yisrael was given a "certificate of divorce" by YHWH because of her backsliding and committing adultery by whoring after other gods.[56]

In order to be restored in her relationship with YHWH someone had to die to pay the price for breaking the Covenant. The death of one of the parties was also required because the Torah forbids remarrying after the parties have

---

[54] "¹ There shall come forth a Rod from the stem of Jesse, and a Branch shall grow out of his roots. ² The Spirit of YHWH shall rest upon Him, The Spirit of wisdom and understanding, The Spirit of counsel and might, The Spirit of knowledge and of the fear of YHWH." Isaiah 11:1-2

[55] Religions, denominations and cults are good at controlling the behavior of their adherents. While on the outside it may appear that the people are walking in unity and truth, if their actions are not motivated by a love of the Commandments, their works are to no avail.

[56] Jeremiah 3:8

been divorced and one of the parties has been defiled.[57]

This was a pattern revealed through the blood covenant process conducted with Abram.[58] Abram was put into a "deep sleep" and only YHWH passed through the pieces of the Covenant signifying that He would bear the punishment for breaking the Covenant. So death was not only required for the house of Yisrael and the house of Judah breaking the Covenant, it was also required so that the house of Yisrael could be restored and remarried to YHWH.

The house of Yisrael needs a covenant renewal ceremony. That will occur in the future through a marriage covenant consummated by a great wedding feast. Again, this is why Yahushua's first recorded miracle was at a wedding and His parables often involved a wedding. He was setting the stage for His ministry and teaching people how to get to that wedding feast in the future.

The Messiah did not come to form a new entity called the Church. Rather, He came to restore Yisrael according to the many promises provided through the prophets. If it wasn't clear enough, Yahushua specifically stated that He came looking for *"the lost sheep of the house of Yisrael"*.[59]

He chose fishermen to literally become fishers of men.[60] As He casts His net looking for the lost sheep He will draw those from the nations who desire to join in the Renewed Covenant with Him. This is how YHWH will use Yisrael to accomplish His purpose.

The word "church" was another invention of the English language and inserted in the New Testament whenever the word "ekklesia" (ἐκκλησία) was found in the Greek texts. "Ekklessia" means: "the set apart Assembly of Elohim" and has the same meaning as the Hebrew word "qahal" (ﻉﺍﻕ) used to refer to the Assembly of Yisrael. So

---

[57] Deuteronomy 24:4
[58] See Genesis 15
[59] Matthew 15:24
[60] Matthew 4:19 and Mark 1:17

there is no such thing as a "church" separate and apart from the Assembly of Yisrael. The "ekklesia" is Yisrael.

The simple fact is that the Messiah is not looking to populate His Kingdom with people who simply answered an altar call or uttered a scripted prayer at some point in their past. Those who believe such a notion have entirely missed the point of the Covenant plan described through the Scriptures.

I spent much of my life in a Christian culture that was obsessed with numbers. Many acted as if the number of "souls that they won" determined their status in heaven. The focus was on the quantity and not necessarily the quality of those conversions.

This can have devastating consequences because the person converting does not necessarily understand that they are entering into a Covenant. We see the results of this evangelistic approach in many of the mega churches found throughout the world. Their messages are often watered down to such an extent that they resemble motivational seminars or rock concerts more than places where people worship YHWH and learn His Torah. They do this to attract more people because the focus is often on growth. Greater numbers is often equated with successful ministeries, but that can be very misleading.

The point of evangelism is not to save everybody, but rather to "fish" for His scattered sheep and draw them back into a Covenant relationship (Jeremiah 16:16). The Messiah is looking for people who will deny themselves and follow him to the death.

"If anyone serves Me, let him follow Me; and where I am, there My servant will be also. If anyone serves Me, him My Father will honor."
John 12:26

"Then He said to them all, 'If anyone desires to come after Me,

let him deny himself, and take up his execution stake daily, and follow Me.'"
Luke 9:23
(see also Matthew 6:24 and Mark 8:34)

The reason for this level of commitment is that it demonstrates that the person loves YHWH and trusts in His promises and the work of His Son. It also unequivocally reveals that they believe in the resurrection, which is the key to our salvation. Remember that Yahushua the Messiah did not just believe, He walked out the Word. If we are to follow Him, then we are also supposed to obey the Commandments.

It is obvious that following the Messiah involves more than making an internal decision. It is a way of life. This highlights the difference between the eastern way of thinking and the western mindset. The Covenant described in the Scriptures was established in an eastern culture involving concrete thought and action. Western thinking is very different – it is abstract.

To an eastern thinking person, the Covenant is a relationship that involves responsibilities, actions and penalties. Eastern thought is very cyclical and the relationship continues through the change in seasons and the cycles of time – it is a process.

To a western thinker, unfamiliar with ancient covenants, the perceptions and interpretations are much different. Westerners think very linear and look at things from one point to another - how to get from point A to point Z.

While the "salvation" described in the Scriptures often meant being delivered from one's enemies, in Christianity it almost always means going to heaven. These are two very different things.

While the Scriptures focus on how people lived their lives here on earth and how they related to Elohim through their struggles, the primary goal of Christianity is to skip all of that and go straight to the dessert – eternal life and heaven. That way of thinking is epitomized by the popular rapture teaching that currently permeates much of modern western Christianity.

Those who believe in the rapture typically think that they will avoid all tribulation by being "raptured" or "removed" from the face of the earth. This notion is completely inconsistent with history and the Scriptures, which reveal how YHWH delivers His people through tribulation, not necessarily from tribulation.[61] Sadly, it is consistent with a society and culture obsessed with self and entertainment.

So many Christian pastors and evangelists have adapted their presentation of salvation to suit the desires of their western audience. They get right to the point, which is consistent with the western linear thought process. They solve the problem of how to get a person from a sinner on their way to hell to a saint with a ticket to heaven with a simple prayer. They have an immediate solution.

Now don't get me wrong; prayer and repentance are both critical steps in the right direction, but they are only the beginning – not the end. They are the entrance to the Covenant path established by the Creator.

Here is what the Messiah had to say about eternal life.

"*2 Since You have given Him authority over all flesh, that He should give eternal life to as many as You have given Him. 3 And this is eternal life, that they may know You, the only true Elohim, and Messiah Yahushua whom You have sent.*"
John 17:2-3

---

[61] The best example of this was when YHWH plagued Egypt. The Yisraelites were not delivered from Egypt until after the plagues were completed, but they were protected through the plagues. So while YHWH was judging Pharaoh and Egypt, His people were protected from those plagues.

Thus eternal life is given to those who know Him, and that involves a relationship, which is defined through the Covenant. In other words, if we want to know Him, we need to do what He says and live according to His Commandments.

The Scriptures actually provide two accounts of when the Messiah was specifically asked the question: "What must I do to inherit eternal life?"

The first time, the question was posed by a Scribe - an expert in the Torah.

"*25 And behold, a certain Scribe stood up and tested Him, saying, 'Teacher, what shall I do to inherit eternal life?' 26 He said to him, 'What is written in the Law (Torah)? What is your reading of it?' 27 So he answered and said, 'You shall love YHWH your Elohim with all your heart, with all your soul, with all your strength, and with all your mind, and your neighbor as yourself.' 28 And He said to him, 'You have answered rightly; do this and you will live.'"*
Luke 10:25-28

The second instance involved a ruler.

"*16 Now behold, one came and said to Him, 'Good Teacher, what good thing shall I do that I may have eternal life?' 17 So He said to him, 'Why do you call Me good? No one is good but One, that is, Elohim. But if you want to enter into life, keep the Commandments.' 18 He said to Him, 'Which ones?' Yahushua said, 'You shall not murder,' 'You shall not commit adultery,' 'You shall not steal,' 'You shall not bear false witness,' 19 'Honor your father and your mother,' and, 'You shall love your neighbor as yourself.' 20 The young man said to Him, 'All these things I have kept from my youth. What do I still lack? 21 Yahushua said to him, 'If you want to be perfect, go, sell what you have and give to the poor, and you will have treasure in heaven; and come, follow Me.'"*
Matthew 19:16-21 (see Luke 18)

In both instances, when asked how a person would inherit eternal life, the Messiah pointed people to the Commandments – the Torah. This response would likely be treated as taboo in modern Christianity.

If a Christian teacher pointed people to the Commandments for eternal life, they would likely be called either 1) legalistic or, 2) a Judaizer, because "the Law" is frowned upon as something that places people in bondage. Again, that is an absurd notion, but it is very prevalent throughout Christianity. Neither of these terms has anything to do with obeying the Commandments, but rather placing the traditions of the Pharisees or any religious denomination or sect over the Torah.

As mentioned previously, "Law" is a word commonly used in English translations of the Scriptures to refer to the Torah, but "Torah" is a Hebrew word that means "instructions". The Torah is essentially the instruction manual, from the Creator to His Creation, embodied in His Commandments. It defines the way we are supposed to live our lives in a manner pleasing to Him. Our obedience is simply an expression of our faith.

The Torah does not place anyone in bondage as implied by the use of the word "Law". Rather, it directs us toward life and blessings and away from the bondage of sin and death.

The Messiah clearly pointed to the Torah as the way to eternal life. This is because it is the righteous instructions of the Torah that point people to Him and help prepare them to live in the eternal Kingdom. If we refuse to acknowledge and follow these righteous instructions now, why should we expect to enter into the Kingdom? The example was provided by the Garden of Eden. Obey and live with Elohim, disobey and be separated from Him.

Now here is the rub - since the Garden we all have sinned and fallen short. We are all sinners and we know this because sin is defined by our failure to obey the

Commandments. We, like Adam and his bride,[62] have disobeyed and deserve to be outside of Paradise.

We all need a perfect sacrifice to atone for, or cover, our sins.[63] But that is just the beginning of the Covenant journey to eternal life. The question is what do we do once we receive that atonement? Do we just keep on sinning? Of course not!

The Book of Hebrews specifically addressed this issue:

> "[26] For if we sin willfully after we have received the knowledge of the truth, there no longer remains a sacrifice for sins, [27] but a certain fearful expectation of judgment, and fiery indignation which will devour the adversaries. [28] Anyone who has rejected Moses' Torah dies without mercy on the testimony of two or three witnesses. [29] Of how much worse punishment, do you suppose, will he be thought worthy who has trampled the Son of Elohim underfoot, counted the blood of the Covenant by which he was sanctified a common thing, and insulted the Spirit of grace?" Hebrews 10:26-29

That is where popular Christian teaching has gone awry. In trying to make the salvation process fast, easy and acceptable to the masses, it distorts the full teaching of the Messiah. The Christian religion generally fails to direct people to the path that the Messiah walked. Instead, they erroneously believe that Messiah walked out the Covenant perfectly so that He could essentially close the door behind Him.

Nothing could be further from the truth. In fact, He

---

[62] The first woman is often called "Eve" but her proper Hebrew name was "Hawah".

[63] Just as the first recorded bride was taken from the DNA of Adam, the Bride Yahushua must be covered, cleansed and transformed by His DNA contained in His blood.

specifically made this statement at the beginning of His ministry. *"17 Do not think that I came to destroy the Torah or the Prophets. I did not come to destroy but to fulfill. 18 For assuredly, I say to you, till heaven and earth pass away, one jot or one tittle will by no means pass from the Torah till all is fulfilled"* Matthew 5:17-18

Despite this clear and unequivocal statement made by the Messiah Himself, many in Christianity believe and teach that the Messiah did away with the Torah. Along with this false doctrine, they typically expound that for a person to actually obey the Commandments is considered "legalism" which then subjects them to bondage. As a result, they are diametrically opposed to the Torah and, likewise, the Covenant.

In order to support the position that the Torah leads to bondage, they typically conclude that the Torah is too difficult. This would make Elohim a sadist and imply that He played some sort of cruel joke by entering into a Covenant with Yisrael that they could not obey.

Of course, that is not the case at all. Moses specifically stated the following to Yisrael before they entered into the Promised Land: *"For this Commandment which I command you today is not too mysterious (difficult) for you, nor is it far off."* Deuteronomy 30:11. He was referring to the Torah.

So there is no confusion or debate, this fact was reiterated in the New Testament. *"For this is the love of Elohim, that we keep His Commandments. And His Commandments are not burdensome."* 1 John 5:3.

This stands in stark contrast to popular Christian teaching and every person must determine whether they will believe a tradition over the Scriptures. Because of unscriptural traditions and teachings, most Christians think that they can receive atonement and then proceed to reject the Torah, ignore and even break the Commandments and still get into the Kingdom of Heaven.

They erroneously believe that they can break the

Commandments and still enter into the Kingdom. This is a grievous mistake based, in large part, on a misunderstood statement made by the Messiah and recorded in Matthew 5:19.

In most English translations of that text we read:

> "Whoever therefore <u>breaks</u> one of the least of these Commandments, and teaches men so, shall be called least in the kingdom of heaven; but whoever does and teaches them, he shall be called great in the kingdom of heaven."

Because of this translation many believe that it is acceptable to break the Commandments. By doing so, you can still make it into the Kingdom, only you will be "least." This begs the question - If you actually believe that those who break the Commandments will be least in the Kingdom, why would you want to settle for least? Why not just obey and be great?

The likely answer is that those who are satisfied with being least are lawless and want to stay that way. In any event, they fail to properly understanding the text. People who knowingly and willfully break the Commandments will not be permitted into the Kingdom of Elohim.[64]

The problem stems from the inaccurate translation of a single word. The operative word in the passage is "breaks", which in the Greek and Aramaic is better translated as "loosen" or "relax". So, this text is not saying that people who break the Commandments will be in the Kingdom, they will not. That has always been the case.

It is people who "loosen" or "relax" the Commandments and teach others to do so who will get in (but just barely) and they will be least in the Kingdom.

This is better understood when you realize that the Torah is often seen as a gentle yoke with cords that help

---

[64] Revelation 22:15

guide us. It is not the yoke of a slave driver.[65] The cords of the Torah guide and direct us, but they must remain fastened in order to feel the tugs from the Creator.

If you loosen the yoke you cannot feel the guiding hand of the Master. The more you loosen the worse it gets until the yoke ultimately comes off.[66]

Those who loosen the Commandments are still obeying the Commandments, but not as diligently as they should. Their hearts are not in it. They are straying from the Tree of Life and drifting toward the Tree of the Knowledge of Good and Evil. If they continue to loosen the Commandments they will eventually end up breaking the Commandments, which results in banishment from the Kingdom.

This truth was demonstrated from the very beginning. It is also confirmed by the context of the passage in Matthew 5. The Messiah had just stated that He did not come to destroy the Torah and the Prophets, but to fulfill. Read His statement again. He could not have been any clearer. *"[17] Do not think that I came to destroy the Torah or the Prophets. I did not come to destroy but to fulfill. [18] For assuredly, I say to you, till heaven and earth pass away, one jot or one tittle will by no means pass from the Torah till all is fulfilled."* Matthew 5:17-18.

Here Yahushua is talking about the absolute validity of the entire Torah and His commitment to live out the Torah. None of it will pass away. All portions are relevant, even the least significant - until heaven and earth pass away. He then goes on to say that, if anyone loosens the Commandments and teaches others to do so, they will be least. Again, they are still obeying, but not as they should be.

Let's take an example of how you might loosen a

---

[65] Hosea 11:4
[66] Once the yoke broken and the bonds are removed there is nothing left to keep the Covenant people from going astray and being destroyed through their transgressions. See Jeremiah 5:4-9.

Commandment. The Sabbath is a clear Commandment. We are to rest on the Sabbath according to the Fourth Commandment.[67] It is actually a sign for all those who are in Covenant with the Creator.[68] The purpose is obvious, so that we can spend time with family, focusing on worship and prayer and study of the Torah.

While there are some well defined restraints in the Scriptures regarding the Sabbath, they are few compared with the myriad of rules, regulations and restrictions imposed by religious traditions.[69] The true purpose is to provide us with rest, not to impose a heavy burden. This is why Yahushua said: "[28] *Come to Me, all you who labor and are heavy laden, and I will give you rest.* [29] *Take My yoke upon you and learn from Me, for I am gentle and lowly in heart, and you will find rest for your souls.* [30] *For My yoke is easy and My burden is light.*" Matthew 11:28-30.

Yahushua opposed the religious leaders as they tried to impose their yoke upon the people, which was heavy and burdensome. The yoke of the Torah was not burdensome.

---

[67] "[8] *Remember the Sabbath day, to keep it holy.* [9] *Six days you shall labor and do all your work,* [10] *but the seventh day is the Sabbath of YHWH your Elohim. In it you shall do no work: you, nor your son, nor your daughter, nor your male servant, nor your female servant, nor your cattle, nor your stranger who is within your gates.* [11] *For in six days YHWH made the heavens and the earth, the sea, and all that is in them, and rested the seventh day. Therefore YHWH blessed the Sabbath day and set it apart.*" Exodus 20:8-11

[68] "*It is a sign between Me and the children of Yisrael forever; for in six days YHWH made the heavens and the earth, and on the seventh day He rested and was refreshed.*" Exodus 31:17

[69] There are likely only seven express or implicit Commandments in the Scriptures concerning the Sabbath. They are not difficult nor are they burdensome. In fact, they are meant to make our lives easy so we truly can rest. Religious traditions have heaped on numerous restrictions and requirements often making the Sabbath a burden to those who are seeking to observe the Sabbath. This is the issue that Yahushua was dealing with through many of His confrontations with the religious leaders. He was teaching the beauty and simplicity of the Torah which had become clouded by religious traditions, rules and regulations imposed by men.

In fact, when Gentiles were repenting and turning to Elohim after the death and resurrection of the Messiah, they were given some basic instructions in righteousness and then they were expected to go to the Synagogue where Moses (the Torah) was read every Sabbath so that they could learn the Torah and fully enter into the Covenant. Here is the instruction that was given: "*For Moses (Torah) has had throughout many generations those who preach him in every city, being read in the synagogues every Sabbath.*"Acts 15:21.

So all those in Covenant with YHWH are expected to observe the Sabbath. Through their obedience they actually display the Sabbath as a sign that they are in Covenant with YHWH. The Sabbath is not something Jewish.[70] It was a special day set apart by the Creator during the first week of our existence. All who join into the Covenant are to carry the Sabbath as a sign. This was clearly expressed by the prophet Isaiah.

> "*1 Thus says YHWH: 'Keep justice, and do righteousness, for My salvation is about to come, and My righteousness to be revealed. 2 Blessed is the man who does this, and the son of man who lays hold on it; who keeps from defiling the Sabbath, and keeps his hand from doing any evil.' 3 Do not let the son of the foreigner who has joined himself to YHWH speak, saying, 'YHWH has utterly separated me from His people;' Nor let the eunuch say, 'Here I am, a dry tree.' 4 For thus says YHWH: 'To the eunuchs who keep My Sabbaths, and choose what pleases Me, and hold fast My Covenant, 5*

---

[70] This is often misunderstood. Neither the religion of Judaism or the Jewish people represent all of Yisrael. At best, they represent the house of Yahudah. The Torah is for all of Yisrael and the Sabbath is a sign for all those in Covenant with YHWH. The restoration of the house of Yisrael is an event anticipated to occur through the Messiah. The restoration of the Kingdom of Yisrael and the identification of the house of Yisrael and the house of Judah is discussed in detail in the Walk in the Light series book entitled *The Redeemed.*

Even to them I will give in My house and within My walls a place and a name better than that of sons and daughters; I will give them an everlasting name that shall not be cut off. ⁶ Also the sons of the foreigner who join themselves to YHWH, to serve Him, and to love the name of YHWH, to be His servants - everyone who keeps from defiling the Sabbath, and holds fast My Covenant ⁷ Even them I will bring to My holy mountain, and make them joyful in My house of prayer. Their burnt offerings and their sacrifices will be accepted on My altar; for My House shall be called a House of prayer for all nations.' ⁸ YHWH Elohim, who gathers the outcasts of Yisrael, says, 'Yet I will gather to him others besides those who are gathered to him.'" Isaiah 56:1-8

It is no coincidence that Yahushua quoted this text when He was cleansing the Temple in Jerusalem.[71] The point is for all to join into the Covenant; this will occur when He gathers the outcasts of Yisrael – all those who have been scattered throughout the world and mixed with the Nations.[72]

Here is the goal of the Sabbath as detailed through the Prophet Isaiah:

---

[71] See Matthew 21:13, Mark 11:17, Luke 19:46

[72] This was aptly demonstrated when Yahushua performed the miracle of the 153 fish after His resurrection. His disciples were supposed to be fishing for the lost sheep of the house of Yisrael (Matthew 10:6). Instead, they were fishing for fish. He told them to cast their nets on the right side of their boats and they gathered in 153 large fish. The number 153 equals the Hebrew phrase "sons of Elohim" which is a reference to the regathering of the house of Yisrael in Hosea 1:10. Those from the house of Judah had neglected the fact that all of Yisrael was to gather and worship at the Temple. They had excluded the nations and constructed a wall of separation that the Gentiles could not cross. With their laws and traditions, they had developed barriers that were in direct opposition to the Torah. This has continued through the laws and traditions handed down from the Pharisees to the religion of Judaism, which generally fails to recognize the current restoration of the house of Yisrael that is drawing the Nations back to the Covenant through the Messiah.

"[13] If you turn away your foot from the Sabbath, from doing your pleasure on My holy day, and call the Sabbath a delight, the holy day of YHWH honorable, and shall honor Him, not doing your own ways, nor finding your own pleasure, nor speaking your own words, [14] Then you shall delight yourself in YHWH; and I will cause you to ride on the high hills of the earth, and feed you with the heritage of Jacob your father. The mouth of YHWH has spoken."
Isaiah 58:13-14

We are supposed to call the Sabbath a delight. It is an incredible day if we don't seek our own pleasures. Now let's say that a person stays home on the Sabbath and does not work. They are obeying the Commandment that is intended to give us the time we need to pray, worship and study the Word. If that is what they are doing and they continue in that direction they will begin to see the delight promised by Isaiah. They are headed in the right direction - closer to Elohim.

Now what if someone comes along and says that it is alright to watch movies all day, surf the internet or play tennis, since that's not really work – it's fun.[73]

That person is definitely "relaxing" the Commandment. They are leading people away from the true intent of the Commandment instead of toward the goal of the Commandment. If you go down that path it will most likely lead to breaking the Commandment altogether.

The text in Matthew 5:19 has nothing to do with people who do not follow the Commandments. It is a warning directed at people who loosen them, which leads

---

[73] The point is not to come up with a list of dos and don'ts. It is about forging a relationship with the Creator and using this special, set apart day, to nurture that relationship. Some would argue that some or all of these examples are actually breaking the Commandment. The subject of the Sabbath is discussed further in the Walk in the Light series book entitled *The Sabbath*.

away from the true intent and purpose and ultimately away from Elohim.

The relationship required by the Creator is established and perfected in the Covenant described in the Scriptures. The Covenant defines our conduct through the Commandments and failure to abide by the terms of the Covenant is called lawlessness.

6

Lawlessness

Clearly, you do not get into the Kingdom if you are a lawless person.[74] In fact, when asked if only a few would be saved the Messiah answered in the affirmative. Here is the passage from Luke:

"*23 Then one said to Him, 'Master, are there few who are saved?' And He said to them, 24 Strive to enter through the narrow gate, for many, I say to you, will seek to enter and will not be able. 25 When once the Master of the house has risen up and shut the door, and you begin to stand outside and knock at the door, saying, 'Lord, Lord, open for us,' and He will answer and say to you, 'I do not know you, where you are from,' 26 then you will begin to say, 'We ate and drank in Your presence, and You taught in our streets.' 27 But He will say, 'I tell you I do not know you, where you are from. Depart from Me, all you workers of iniquity.' 28 There will be weeping and*

---

[74] Yahushua made this very clear when He likened the Kingdom to a wedding feast. "*11 But when the king came in to see the guests, he saw a man there who did not have on a wedding garment. 12 So he said to him, 'Friend, how did you come in here without a wedding garment?' And he was speechless. 13 Then the king said to the servants, 'Bind him hand and foot, take him away, and cast him into outer darkness; there will be weeping and gnashing of teeth.' 14 For many are called, but few are chosen.*" Matthew 22:11-14. It is very clear that those attending the wedding in the Kingdom must be clean "*not having spot or wrinkle or any such thing, but that she should be holy and without blemish.*" Ephesians 5:27. You must be cleansed by the blood of the Lamb to attend the Marriage Supper of the Lamb and, after receiving that cleansing, you must remain clean by living righteously. "*And to her it was granted to be arrayed in fine linen, clean and bright, for the fine linen is the righteous acts of the saints.*" Revelation 19:8. Righteous conduct is not something mysterious. It is defined in the Torah.

gnashing of teeth, when you see Abraham and Isaac and Jacob and all the prophets in the Kingdom of Elohim, and yourselves thrust out." Luke 13:23-28

According to the Messiah many will try to get into the Kingdom, but the Master does not know them because they are defined as "workers of iniquity". They are the opposite of those who work righteousness.

Remember that righteousness and sin are defined through the Torah. Obedience is righteousness and disobedience is lawlessness. The workers of iniquity are lawless individuals who have refused to take on the yoke of the Torah and labor for the Kingdom. They work iniquity instead of righteousness.

As previously mentioned, a popular tagline used in Christianity is that you need to know Jesus as "your personal Lord and Savior." The focus to this approach is placed on the individual, when YHWH typically speaks about saving His people. There is clearly a ring of truth to this statement though, since we will all stand before Him some day and give an account. It is critical to understand that our relationship status is provided through the Covenant.

Ultimately, our fate depends upon whether Yahushua knows us and whether we know Him. He made it abundantly clear that our relationship is defined by our conduct, not simply a decision that we made at some point in our lives. And it is not the actions that we think we should do, but rather, what He commands us to do.

Those who refuse to do what He commands are defined as lawless, and the lawless ones do not get into the Kingdom – not even those who claim to be prophets. They do not have a "personal relationship" with Him as Lord and Savior, even though they think they do.

This statement should give pause to most Christians:

"¹³ Enter by the narrow gate; for wide is the gate and broad is the way that leads to destruction, and there are many who go in

by it. *14 Because narrow is the gate and difficult is the way which leads to life, and there are few who find it. 15 'Beware of false prophets, who come to you in sheep's clothing, but inwardly they are ravenous wolves. 16 You will know them by their fruits. Do men gather grapes from thorn bushes or figs from thistles? 17 Even so, every good tree bears good fruit, but a bad tree bears bad fruit. 18 A good tree cannot bear bad fruit, nor can a bad tree bear good fruit. 19 Every tree that does not bear good fruit is cut down and thrown into the fire. 20 Therefore by their fruits you will know them. 21 Not everyone who says to Me, 'Lord, Lord,' shall enter the kingdom of heaven, but he who does the will of My Father in heaven. 22 Many will say to Me in that day, 'Lord, Lord, have we not prophesied in Your name, cast out demons in Your name, and done many wonders in Your name?' 23 And then I will declare to them, 'I never knew you; depart from Me, you who practice lawlessness!'"* Matthew 7:13-23

Those who practice lawlessness are those "without the Torah." They are the ones who do not follow the Commandments. He does not know those who do not follow His Commandments. In other words, He does not have a relationship with those people. It does not matter what you say or do if you are not bearing good fruit by obeying the Commandments.

The Commandments are at the heart of the Covenant and the Covenant defines the relationship between Elohim and mankind. You are not in a relationship with Him if you are not in Covenant with Him. As a result, if you think or state that you have a relationship with the Messiah outside the Covenant or the Commandments you are mistaken. You may find yourself in that group of "many" described by the Messiah.

If you think that you can just say a prayer and then disregard the Commandments then you are deceived. In fact, the Scriptures go so far as to call you a liar if you say such a thing. *"He who says, 'I know Him,' and does not keep His Commandments, is a liar, and the truth is not in him."* 1 John 2:4.

The standard for knowing Him is clear. *"Now by this we know that we know Him, if we keep His Commandments."* 1 John 2:3.

This fact is made abundantly clear throughout the Scriptures. If you refuse to obey you do not get into the Kingdom. Further, if you are in the Kingdom and decide not to obey you get ejected from the Kingdom.

"The Son of Man will send out His angels, <u>and they will gather out of His Kingdom all things that offend, and those who practice lawlessness</u>." Matthew 13:41

These lawless ones likely started by loosening the Commandments, which ultimately led to them breaking the Commandments. They will not remain in the Kingdom. This is at the very heart of our discussion on salvation because the point is to enter through the narrow gate that leads to life.[75] This involves a return to the Garden where we find fellowship with our Creator – the source of life. The Hebrew word for "garden" is "gan" (גן) and it means: "an enclosed or protected space." The Garden of Eden was hedged in by the Commandments.[76]

Sadly, most religions fail to understand or represent the principles of the Kingdom. This should be no surprise. The Messiah claimed that rampant lawlessness would be a sign of the end. *"And because lawlessness will abound, the love of many will grow cold."* Matthew 24:12. Notice that lawlessness is directly linked with the lack of love for Elohim, and remember that love is directly connected with obedience.[77]

Our actions define and demonstrate our love or lack thereof. There are many who claim to love God or Jesus, but their actions reveal who they are truly serving. If they reject the Torah and are living lives of lawlessness then they do not love Yahushua. They love themselves, their religion, their

---

[75] Matthew 7:14

[76] The Garden represented the Kingdom of YHWH. The Commandments are the rule of the Kingdom. That is why the man and the woman were expelled from the Kingdom. They "broke the law" and were punished.

[77] John 14:15 and 15:10

religious leaders or their traditions.

The Messiah specifically said: "*[23] If anyone loves Me, he will keep My word; and My Father will love him, and We will come to him and make Our home with him. [24] He who does not love Me does not keep My words; and the word which you hear is not Mine but the Father's who sent Me.*" John 14:23-24

There is no mistake, the Word of Yahushua is the same as the Word of YHWH. The Commandments of Yahushua are the same as the Commandments of YHWH. There is no distinction or difference between the two. Yahushua said ". . . *he who has seen me has seen the Father . . .*" John 14:9. He also said: "*I and the Father are one.*" John 10:30. He was the Word from the beginning[78] and He never changed the Torah by fulfilling the prophecies and renewing the Covenant.

Thus, as people increasingly reject His Word (the Torah), their love grows cold. As they continue in lawlessness, they stray farther and farther from Him. Again, the Commandments are like a gentle yoke. They steer and guide us in the right direction. When our lives are guided by the Commandments, we will be productive servants, plowing the fallow ground so that the seeds of the Kingdom can be planted and the Kingdom can grow and bear fruit through the righteous ones.

If we refuse to go the way of the Commandments, but instead choose our own path, we will be of no use to the King. We will be cut down and thrown into the fire. This is what Yahsshua said so you should not be shocked by this message. This is exactly what He was referring to when He rejected the lawless ones. They are *many* who are doing what they want instead of what He commands. There is no denying that this group of *many* people sounds exactly like the modern Christian Church. In fact, there really is no other group of people on Earth that fits the description.

---

[78] See John 1

Those in the Christian religion specifically claim to follow the Messiah, but many do not really know Him. They do not even know His Name. They certainly do not love Him if they refuse to obey His Commandments. Many are serving a fictional christ that advocates lawlessness. They also rely on an erroneous understanding of "grace"[79] for salvation while rejecting and neglecting the terms of the Covenant that provides salvation and deliverance.

The Messiah was very clear when He stated: "[29] *Take My yoke upon you and learn from Me, for I am gentle and lowly in heart, and you will find rest for your souls. [30] For My yoke is easy and My burden is light.*" Matthew 11:29-30

Sadly, most Christians interpret this passage to mean that the yoke of the Torah was too difficult for men to bear, as if the Father is a cruel slave driver, placing a burden upon Yisrael that was too heavy to bear. So cruel was the Father that the Son had to come and remove that burden and give us a lighter one. This is a twisted and perverted understanding of Elohim. It infiltrated Christianity through an ancient heretic named Marcion from the second century of the Common Era.[80]

---

[79] Grace is one of the most abused doctrines in Christianity. The word "grace" literally means: "thanks". What Christians refer to as "grace" is better described as "mercy" or "favor". It is the idea that we receive something that we do not deserve and this, of course, describes the work of the Messiah through His death and resurrection. Christianity then extends this notion of grace to conclude that there is nothing that we can do after receiving the free gift. They believe that the Torah was bondage and that by grace we have been released from bondage and are now free to do whatever we please. This is similar to the satanic doctrine espoused by Aleister Crowley that states: "Do what thou wilt." This is the epitome of lawlessness. The subject of grace is described in detail in the Walk in the Light series book entitled *The Law and Grace*.

[80] Marcion of Sinope lived between 85 CE and 160 CE. He was the Bishop of a heretical religious sect referred to as the Marcionites. He taught a dualist belief system that the god of the Old Testament was a separate and distinct god from the one in the New Testament. As a result, he emphasized various texts over the Old Testament and essentially threw

His yoke was always easy. In fact, He is the one who delivers His people from bondage and slavery. He relieves His people from the heavy yoke of the slavemaster and the burdens that religions and the traditions of men place upon us. In the passage in Matthew 11, Yahushua was referring specifically to Hosea 11. It describes how YHWH gently guided Yisrael, as a father would a child.

"*¹ When Yisrael was a child, I loved him, and out of Egypt I called My son. ² As they called them, so they went from them; They sacrificed to the Baals, and burned incense to carved images. ³ I taught Ephraim to walk, taking them by their arms; but they did not know that I healed them. ⁴ I drew them with gentle cords, with bands of love, and I was to them as those who take the yoke from their neck. I stooped and fed them.*" Hosea 11:1-4

Ephraim was the leading tribe from the house of Yisrael and therefore often represented the house of Yisrael after the Kingdom was divided.[81] The Creator does not oppress us with a heavy burden. Rather, He gently guides us.[82] Notice the tenderness that YHWH demonstrated to His

out the foundation of the faith. Because of the destructive nature of his false teachings, many attribute the decision to develop the canon of the New Testament to Marcion. The development of the canon of the New Testament was essentially an attempt to solidify orthodox doctrine and agree upon texts that supported that doctrine. Prior to that time, various letters and Gospels were circulating amongst the Assemblies, and were not treated as Scriptures. For an indepth discussion of the debelopment of the Bible see the Walk in the Light series book entitled *The Scriptures*.

[81] Because of the egregious sins of Solomon, YHWH took 10 tribes away from his kingdom after his death. The 10 Northern Tribes referred to as the house of Yisrael were given to the reign of Jeroboam from the Tribe of Ephraim. The tribes of Judah and Benjamin, called the Southern Tribes and the house of Judah were retained by Rehoboam, the son of Solomon. This process is described in 1 Kings 11-12. Very interestingly, Ephraim is often symbolized as a bull or an ox - a powerful animal with horns. If Ephraim takes on the yoke of the Master and allows himself to be directed he can be a powerful force for the Kingdom. Left unrestrained he can cause great destruction.

[82] The purpose is to keep us on the Ancient Path of the righteous way so that we can find rest for our souls. See Jeremiah 6:16.

children. He lovingly directs us to Him.

The difficulty comes when we are surrounded by the nations and drawn to their false gods and idols. We also get burdened by laws, rules, regulations and traditions heaped upon us by religions. The Commandments themselves are certainly not too difficult to obey. In fact, it is the Commandments that provide rest.[83]

Recall that this was specifically stated by Moses after he spoke the words of the Covenant before the people entered into the Promised Land. *"For this Commandment which I command you today is not too mysterious for you, nor is it far off."* Deuteronomy 30:11

Some translations state: *"it is not too difficult."* In other words, it can be known and it can be done. He isn't saying that it won't be difficult, just not too difficult.[84]

Remember that this was also specifically stated in the New Testament. *"For this is the love of Elohim, that we keep His Commandments. And His Commandments are not burdensome."* 1 John 5:3

So how can so many people be deceived in the end? The answer, in large part, rests on their belief. They have chosen to believe a lie that directs them to lawless conduct despite the clear instructions and warnings of the Messiah.

---

[83] Remember that the Fourth Commandment provides us with rest every seventh day – this applies to servants, slaves and even animals. The Torah also provides rest for the Land every seventh year, known as the Shemitah Year. After the seventh Shemitah Year there is an additional year of rest known as the Jubilee Year. Obviously if the Land is resting the people are not plowing and sowing so there is an incredible grant of rest to the people from their labors. This phenomenon, which is unheard of in the history of agricultural societies, demonstrates the nature of YHWH and his desire to bless and provide rest for His people.

[84] Interestingly, the life of Moses is a good example of the fact that sin has consequences. Moses was a great prophet and had an exceptional status in the eyes of YHWH. Because of the great honor and privilege afforded to him, much was expected. When he failed to diligently obey the Command of YHWH, his disobedience enraged YHWH and resulted in punishment. Moses was not allowed into the Promised Land.

They have also believed various twisted Scripture passages that supposedly support their doctrine of lawlessness. Let us now examine the source and arguments for that false belief.

7

Belief

With the foundation of salvation having been laid by the Messiah, let us now look at other statements found in the Scriptures that provide instruction concerning salvation. When asked the question: "What must I do to be saved?" Paul responded: "*Believe on the Lord Jesus Christ (Yahushua Messiah), and you will be saved, you and your household.*" Acts 16:31

This simple passage is loaded with information and requirements. First, you must "believe". From a western perspective, that is typically understood to constitute an internal thought or decision. From an eastern perspective, belief is demonstrated by your actions.

For instance, many people state that they believe in God, as if that "belief" alone actually means something. James succinctly addressed that notion when he proclaimed: "*[19] You believe that there is one Elohim. You do well. Even the demons believe - and tremble! [20] But do you want to know, O foolish man, that faith without works is dead?*" James 2:19-20. He went on to state: "*You see then that a man is justified by works, and not by faith only.*" James 2:24. So he equated faith with belief, but stated that we are "justified" by works and not faith alone.

The Greek word for "justified" is "dikayo'o" (δικαιοῦται) and it means "to be righteous". What James is saying is that belief alone does not make you righteous. It is belief coupled with obedience to the Commandments.

So your belief is something that you live. You exhibit your belief by how you act. Now that ties directly with the title "Lord", which means "Master". If you are a servant, then you obey your master. You do what He says.

In order to obey your Master you must know Him. Part of knowing Him involves properly identifying His

Name so that you can discern what He taught and commanded. Again, the English word Jesus is actually the Hebrew Name Yahushua, and the Greek title Christ should basically be rendered as the word Messiah, which in Hebrew is Moshiach.

Knowing and believing in the proper Name is important because with the Name comes the authority to save and it defines the true Master.[85] So if the Messiah named Yahushua is your Master, then you do as He says and that determines whether or not you really believe in Him.

Now the quote from Paul in Acts 16:31 is the basis for the popular sinner's prayer formula, but sadly most do not glean its true meaning. In his letter to the Romans, Paul wrote the following: *"if you confess with your mouth the Lord Jesus (Master Yahushua) and believe in your heart that God (Elohim) has raised Him from the dead, you will be saved."* Romans 10:9

Here we have a similar formula involving confessing the Master Yahushua. From an eastern perspective it involves not just saying it, but doing it. When you make someone master you do what they say. Yahushua said: *"If you love Me, keep My Commandments."* John 14:15

So if Yahushua is truly your Master you obey the Commandments, especially if you want to express your love for Him. His Commandments are definitely the same Commandments found in the Old Testament, and this tends to scare most Christians.

Again, they mistakenly equate obedience to the Commandments with legalism and bondage. They generally perceive the Old Testament as old, outdated, abolished, and often irrelevant since they identify themselves with the Church, rather than Yisrael. The problem is that the only Covenant Assembly in a relationship with YHWH is

---

[85] Yahushua said: *"He who believes in Him is not condemned; but he who does not believe is condemned already, because he has not believed in the name of the only begotten Son of Elohim."* John 3:18.

Yisrael, not the Christian Church.[86]

The Commandments are absolutely relevant to the people in Covenant with Elohim. Somehow, Christians think that since there is no standing Temple, the Torah is no longer valid. Of course, this belief is in direct contradiction to the statement Yahushua made when He said that as long as heaven and earth remain, so does the Torah.[87] The Torah contains the instructions that apply to us in this present physical creation.

While there were times in the past when the Temple was destroyed, that in no way impacted people's obligation to obey the Torah. There are certain Commandments that apply to the Priesthood and the Temple Service. Those could not be physically kept without an operating Altar, but many of the Commandments simply instruct us how to live.[88]

Those in Covenant with YHWH continue to follow the instructions that apply to them. They still circumcise their children on the eighth day. They still observe the Sabbath each week and the Appointed Times throughout the year. They still eat only the diet prescribed by the Creator, and they still refrain from sexual deviancy.

Sadly, the moral deterioration in the so-called

---

[86] The Christian Church is actually a fictitious entity created by the Roman Catholic Church and perpetuated by the English language. As previously mentioned in Footnote 11, the word "qahal" in Hebrew, which refers to the set apart assembly of Yisrael, shares the same meaning as the Greek word "ekklesia" which is often translated as "church" in the English language. People only read the English word "church" in the New Testament and they do not see it in the Old Testament. As a result, they assume that the Church must have replaced Yisrael, since Yisrael is barely mentioned in the New Testament. What they fail to realize is that the ekklesia is Yisrael. The notion that the Christian Church replaced Yisrael stems from a false doctrine called Replacement Theology.

[87] Matthew 5:17

[88] Even the Commandments relating to the Priesthood and the Temple have significance to everyone. If you want to live and serve in the Kingdom of YHWH you need to understand how He operates His House.

Christian nation of America is due in large part to the confused understanding of the Commandments in Christianity. The entire moral code for mankind is found in the Torah.

Instead of teaching the Torah, Christianity teaches lawlessness and, as a result, the Christian Church has separated herself from the set apart assembly of Yisrael and fallen into the role of the harlot described in the Book of Revelation, also known as Mystery Babylon.[89] The Christian Church claims to be the Bride of Christ, but she is a prostitute. She is lawless and unfaithful, doing the bidding of the lawless one by deceiving the sheep and chasing after false gods.[90] Is it any wonder then that the Christian nation of America has fallen so far?

Yahushua actually spent a great deal of time teaching the Torah. In fact, when asked what was the greatest Commandment He declared: "[29] *The first of all the Commandments is: 'Hear, O Yisrael, YHWH our Elohim, YHWH is One.* [30] *And you shall love YHWH your Elohim with all your heart, with all your soul, with all your mind, and with all your strength.' This is the first Commandment.*" Mark 12:29-30

The observant reader will also recall that this was the same response that Yahushua affirmed would lead to eternal life.[91] Of course, this is the most important prayer in Yisrael known as "The Shema." It is found in Deuteronomy 6:4-5. He then went on to state: "*And the second, like it, is this: You shall love your neighbor as yourself.' There is no other Commandment greater than these.*" Mark 12:31. Here He was quoting Leviticus 19:18

Yahushua was not nullifying or changing the

---

[89] The identity of Mystery Babylon is discussed in detail in the Walk in the Light series book entitled *The Final Shofar*.

[90] The infiltration of pagan practices into the Christian religion is described in greater detail in the Walk in the Light series books entitled *Restoration* and *Pagan Holidays*.

[91] Luke 10:25-28

Commandments as many believe. Rather, He was teaching the true intent of the Torah and affirming that love was at the heart of the Torah. Love perfects the Torah.

That is why Moses promised: *"And YHWH your Elohim will circumcise your heart and the heart of your descendants, to love YHWH your Elohim with all your heart and with all your soul, that you may live."* Deuteronomy 30:6

Now back to the quote from Paul in Romans. The second portion of Romans 10:9 includes belief, as we read in Acts 16:31. Paul says to believe in your heart that Elohim raised Yahushua from the dead. Again, when you truly believe something in your heart that belief does not remain inside, it is expressed by your external actions.

This is the circumcision of the heart spoken of by Moses that would be accomplished through the Renewed Covenant prophesied by Jeremiah. It is the inscribing of the Torah on our hearts so that the Commandments course through our veins. It transforms our DNA and we live the Torah just as Yahushua was the living Torah. This is how we love Elohim with all our heart, with all our soul, with all our mind and all our strength.

This is what it means to be "born again". Flesh cannot inherit the Kingdom. Yahushua said: *"Most assuredly, I say to you, unless one is born of water and the Spirit, he cannot enter the kingdom of Elohim."* John 3:5

The Spiritual rebirth and renewal was prophesied by Ezekiel. *"I will give you a renewed heart and put a renewed spirit within you; I will take the heart of stone out of your flesh and give you a heart of flesh."* Ezekiel 36:26. The connection between the Torah and the Spirit in this rebirthing process was made evident on the Appointed Time of Pentecost.[92] Our belief

---

[92] Pentecost, also known as Shavuot, was the Day that the Torah was spoken forth from Mount Sinai in an awesome display. It was also the day when tongues of fire appeared and the Spirit filled many in Jerusalem who then spoke the words in diverse tongues. The fact that these events

must involve receiving the Spirit and a new heart so that we can truly obey.

We already mentioned what James had to say about belief. He was the brother of Yahushua and the undisputed leader of the Assembly in Jerusalem.[93] Here is his position again in full context:

> "[18] . . . someone will say, 'You have faith, and I have works.' Show me your faith without your works, and I will show you my faith by my works. [19] You believe that there is one Elohim. You do well. Even the demons believe - and tremble! [20] But do you want to know, O foolish man, that faith without works is dead? [21] Was not Abraham our father justified by works when he offered Isaac his son on the altar? [22] Do you see that faith was working together with his works, and by works faith was made perfect? [23] And the Scripture was fulfilled which says, 'Abraham believed Elohim, and it was accounted to him for righteousness.' And he was called the friend of Elohim. [24] You see then that a man is justified by works, and not by faith only. [25] Likewise, was not Rahab the harlot also justified by works when she received the messengers and sent them out another way? [26] For as the body without the spirit is dead, so faith without works is dead also." James 2:18-26

Basically, James says: "show me your faith and I'll show you my works." He is stating that if you truly believe something, you will act according to your belief. If you believe that you were a sinner because you transgressed the

---

occurred on the same Appointed Time is no coincidence. The Spirit and the Torah are not in opposition, rather they are integral to one another.

[93] While Christianity places great emphasis on Paul, there is no question that James, the brother of Yahushua, was the undisputed leader of the Assembly of Believers in Jerusalem. This is apparent from Acts 15 when a matter was brought before the Jerusalem Council and James decided the matter. It is also evident from numerous early historical writings.

Torah and believe that you are forgiven and cleansed by the blood of the Messiah, then you clearly will not continue to sin any longer. If you truly believe in the Messiah, the Word made flesh, then you will obey the Word.

In another poignant statement from James we read the following: "²² But be doers of the word, and not hearers only, deceiving yourselves. ²³ For if anyone is a hearer of the word and not a doer, he is like a man observing his natural face in a mirror; ²⁴ for he observes himself, goes away, and immediately forgets what kind of man he was. ²⁵ But he who looks into the perfect law (Torah) of liberty and continues in it, and is not a forgetful hearer but a doer of the work, this one will be blessed in what he does." James 1:22-25

He really could not have been any clearer. You cannot just hear the word, you must live the word. So many people talk about being obedient to God, but they lack the specificity as to what it means to obey. James refers to the Commandments as the "perfect law of liberty" or better yet "the perfect Torah of liberty." Notice how he equates the Commandments and obedience with liberty, which is the exact opposite of slavery and bondage.

We must hear <u>and</u> obey, and that is the meaning of the Hebrew word "shema" (שְׁמַע) - "hear and obey". Therefore your works, or rather your obedience to the Commandments, will set you free and reflect your true belief. Your obedience will result in blessings. On the other hand, if you fail to obey the Commandments after confessing belief then your belief is dead or non-existent.

So belief in Yahushua is not simply belief that He existed at some point in history. You believe that He was the Word of Elohim manifested in the flesh - the Torah in the flesh. You believe what He taught and you do what He taught. Your actions will demonstrate your belief. If you obey His Commands then you believe Him. If you are lawless then you do not believe in Him. That is the essence of belief, yet some continue to disregard the Torah because they misinterpret the writings of Paul.

8

Paul

Paul summed up the subject of salvation by stating that if you confess the Master Yahushua and believe in the resurrection, then you will be saved. It should be clear by now that this involves much more than an internal decision, a simple prayer or a confession of faith. It involves a life of following the Messiah and walking out the Torah.

Also, Paul did not say that you were immediately saved, but rather that you will be saved. In other words, if you live your life in such a way that evidences your belief then, when you stand before His throne, you will not be cast aside. Rather, you will receive the atonement provided by the shed blood of the Messiah and you will be saved from the punishment of separation and death that you deserve. Instead by grace, better known as mercy, you will be granted entrance into the Kingdom.

Thus, salvation is a future event; it is not something that happens when we say a prayer. This is repeatedly confirmed through many statements made by Paul.

We will focus on Paul a bit more at this point because his writings are often used by Christians to justify their lawlessness.[94] Indeed, some scholars assert that Paul actually founded the Christian religion because they recognize the influence that his writings have had on the religion of Christianity.

When examining the writings of Paul that are included in the Bible, it is important to understand that they are letters to various groups of people and, as a result, they are one sided conversations dealing with specific issues involving those groups. The letters must be read in context,

---

[94] This subject is discussed further in the Walk in the Light series book entitled The Scriptures.

but often we do not know the entire context.

Consequently, we must be careful about how we interpret and apply those passages. We cannot create new doctrine based upon one-sided conversations. Of course, this was never the intention of the Epistles. They were written to explain the Torah, not change it.

Then, it must be conceded that nothing Paul wrote can contradict the Commandments or the teachings of the Master Yahushua. Otherwise, he would be considered a false prophet. YHWH specifically commanded us not to add to or take away from the Torah.[95] No one is authorized to do such a thing, and the Messiah expressly stated that was not His intention.[96] So if you believe that Paul did such a thing then you have essentially made him your god.

Finally, the letters from Paul often involved complex issues regarding the Torah. Paul was a Torah scholar and for those unfamiliar with the Torah, his words are often misunderstood.[97]

That is why Peter specifically stated: "[14] *Therefore, beloved, looking forward to these things, be diligent to be found by Him in peace, without spot and blameless;* [15] *and consider that the longsuffering of our Master is salvation - as also our beloved brother Paul, according to the wisdom given to him, has written to you,* [16] *as also in all his epistles, speaking in them of these things, in which are some things hard to understand, which untaught and unstable people twist to their own destruction, as they do also the rest of the Scriptures.*" 2 Peter 3:14-16

Here Peter is talking about looking forward to the Day of YHWH and our future. In this context he encourages

---

[95] "*You shall not add to the word which I command you, nor take from it, that you may keep the commandments of YHWH your Elohim which I command you.*" Deuteronomy 4:2

[96] Matthew 5:17

[97] Paul described himself as follows: "*I am indeed a Jew, born in Tarsus of Cilicia, but brought up in this city at the feet of Gamaliel, taught according to the strictness of our fathers' law, and was zealous toward Elohim as you all are today.*" Acts 22:3

the reader to be diligent to be found without spot and blameless. Clearly, he is telling people to diligently obey the righteous instructions in the Torah.

He is actually interpreting Paul's letters by stating that Paul teaches that the longsuffering of our Master is salvation. In other words, salvation is not immediate, but requires patience and endurance. He also warned that Paul's letters were hard to understand and that untaught and unstable people were twisting Paul's words to their own destruction

Disregarding this warning, most of Christianity has done exactly that. Many are untaught and do not understand the Torah because they have been told that it is no longer applicable. They then twist Paul's words to justify lawlessness. They do this to their own destruction because that is the end of lawlessness – death and destruction.

You cannot justify lawless behavior through the words of the Messiah or Moses, James, Peter or John – the "pillars" of the Early Assembly"[98] – only Paul. Why anyone would think that one man had the ability to declare that the Torah was abolished is beyond comprehension. It defies all reason and is completely contrary to the Scriptures.

Regardless, the majority of Christians have elevated this man, Paul, above all other prophets, the disciples and even the Messiah by believing that through his letters sent to various groups he had the authority to change the word of Elohim.[99] Most of the time, Paul is simply misquoted or the context of his writing is misunderstood. Therefore, we will examine some of his statements on salvation to see what they

---

[98] Galatians 2:9

[99] When you put this entire argument into perspective it is absurd, but this is what the Christian Church has done. Christianity has essentially elevated Paul, through his misunderstood and misinterpreted letters, to a god-like status. This lopsided view of the texts found in the Bible is detailed more thoroughly in the Walk in the Light series book entitled *The Scriptures.*

actually say.

In Romans 10:13 he states: *"Whoever calls on the Name of YHWH shall be saved."* Here Paul is quoting Joel 2:32 which specifically refers to the Day of YHWH commonly referred to as The Day of the LORD – a future date.

In Romans 11:26 he states: *"And so all Yisrael will be saved, as it is written: 'The Deliverer will come out of Zion, and He will turn away ungodliness from Jacob.'"* He is not talking here about Jews or citizens of the modern State of Israel. Rather, he is talking about the Bride – Yisrael. This is the Covenant assembly of those who follow the Commandments and all Yisrael will indeed be saved in the future.

In 1 Corinthians 5:5 we read: *"deliver such a one to satan for the destruction of the flesh, that his spirit may be saved in the day of the Master Yahushua."* This passage provides that salvation occurs in the Day of the Master Yahushua or the Day of YHWH – a future event.

In 1 Corinthians 15:1-2 we read: *"¹ Moreover, brethren, I declare to you the good news which I preached to you, which also you received and in which you stand, ² by which also you are saved, if you hold fast that word which I preached to you - unless you believed in vain."* Notice here that they are saved - if they hold fast.

In 2 Corinthians 2:15 we read: *"For we are to Elohim the fragrance of Messiah among those who are being saved and among those who are perishing."* Being saved is a process. Those who are being saved are those who are walking according to the Covenant, and those who are perishing are the lawless ones.

Of course, Paul made no mystery of the fact that salvation was a future event when he compared the walk of faith to a race. *"²⁴ Do you not know that those who run in a race all run, but one receives the prize? Run in such a way that you may obtain it. ²⁵ And everyone who competes for the prize is temperate in all things. Now they do it to obtain a perishable crown, but we for an imperishable crown. ²⁶ Therefore I run thus: not with uncertainty. Thus I fight: not as one who beats the air. ²⁷ But I discipline my body and bring it into subjection, lest, when I have preached to others, I myself should become disqualified."* 1 Corinthians 9:24-27

Imagine that! He is suggesting that he could actually become disqualified from the race. That stands in stark contrast to the popular "once saved always saved" doctrine espoused by many Christians. The Greek word used for "disqualified is "adokimos" (ἀδόκιμος) which means: "rejected." He described the walk of faith that leads to salvation as a journey that might not be finished or an objective that might not be achieved. Also note that he is definitely not talking about being least, but rather first.

In his letter to Philemon he encouraged the reader to *"work out your own salvation with fear and trembling"* Philemon 2:12. So, according to Paul, the altar call or prayer of faith is only the entry point to the race. It is not the end, but only the beginning of the journey to salvation. Salvation is a process that must be "worked out" or rather "walked out".

His position should be clear, but many still use various quotes from his letters to support the notion that they do not have to obey the Commandments. The argument usually begins with the following quote from the letter to the Romans. *"For sin shall not have dominion over you, for you are not under law but under grace."* Romans 6:14. They interpret this passage to mean that the Torah does not apply anymore, but that would also mean that there is no longer a definition of sin. The concept is really quite ridiculous.

The Torah is the marriage contract. It is a gift from YHWH that reveals the way of righteousness and blessings for His Bride. You definitely do not want to get rid of the Torah, and that is not what Paul is talking about.

The problem is that most are taught that Paul was advocating the abolition of the Torah and they fail to read the next verse, which clearly states: *"What then? Shall we sin because we are not under law but under grace? Certainly not!"* Romans 6:15. Clearly, we need to be following the

Commandments; otherwise we are sinning.

Paul was simply stating that if you accepted the atonement offered by the Messiah, you are free from sin and no longer subject to the penalty of sin and death. Those who are untaught twist his statements, and those twisted statements lead *many* to destruction because they are lawless.[100]

Another quote of Paul from his letter to the Ephesians is also used to support the notion that the Torah is no longer applicable to Christians. "*8 For by grace you have been saved through faith, and that not of yourselves; it is the gift of Elohim, 9 not of works, lest anyone should boast.*" Ephesians 2:8-9

Here, Paul is simply stating that our salvation comes through the merciful act of the Messiah. We cannot earn our salvation through our works. Even if you obeyed all of the Commandments from this day forward, you still need the atonement that comes from the blood of the Messiah. Of course, if we truly believe in the Messiah and follow His teachings, then we express our faith through our obedience.

In this way we are saved through faith. This becomes clearer when we understand another statement from Paul that: "*faith comes by hearing and hearing by the Word of Elohim.*" Romans 10:17. When we hear the Word it leads to faith. When we live the Word, that faith then becomes real. This is the essence of the word "shema" (שְׁמַע).

So, even from the writings of Paul, which Christians often use to justify breaking the Commandments, it is clear that the Torah is still applicable to those who follow the Messiah.

---

[100] This is why <u>many</u> will be cast away by the Messiah at judgment. "*21 Not everyone who says to Me, 'Lord, Lord,' shall enter the kingdom of heaven, but he who does the will of My Father in heaven. 22 Many will say to Me in that day, 'Lord, Lord, have we not prophesied in Your name, cast out demons in Your name, and done many wonders in Your name?' 23 And then I will declare to them, 'I never knew you; depart from Me, you who practice lawlessness!'*" Matthew 7:21-23

A close reading of His letters reveals that he was often explaining how followers of the Messiah would deal with those Judaizers who taught that salvation came from works alone. This is clearly not the case, it begins with the Messiah and His blood, but salvation is something that comes in the end for those who have demonstrated their belief through their obedience.

9

In the End

In the end, it all comes down to the heart. We must have circumcised hearts to truly obey the Commandments, and this is what the Messiah taught when He proclaimed: "*²⁰ For I say to you, that unless your righteousness exceeds the righteousness of the scribes and Pharisees, you will by no means enter the Kingdom of Heaven. ²¹ You have heard that it was said to those of old, 'You shall not murder, and whoever murders will be in danger of the judgment.' ²² But I say to you that whoever is angry with his brother without a cause shall be in danger of the judgment. And whoever says to his brother, Raca! shall be in danger of the council. But whoever says, 'You fool!' shall be in danger of hell fire . . .²⁷ You have heard that it was said to those of old, 'You shall not commit adultery.' ²⁸ But I say to you that whoever looks at a woman to lust for her has already committed adultery with her in his heart.*" Matthew 5:20-22, 27-28

The Messiah was teaching that obedience transcended mere outward appearance and went straight to the heart. The Pharisees looked like they were obeying the Commandments, but their hearts were not pure. They did not have hearts to obey the Torah, and they often followed their traditions over the Commandments.[101] Because of this, they were declared to be "lawless".

"Even so you also outwardly appear righteous to men, but inside you are full of hypocrisy and lawlessness."
Matthew 23:28

Despite the fact that they appeared to be obeying the Commandment, and were definitely legalistic, they were

---

[101] Matthew 15:3

declared to be lawless. Though their flesh was circumcised, their hearts were not.[102] They were full of sin. How incredible that these were the ones who heaped traditions on men and women – all for naught.

These legalistic religious leaders were still declared lawless because they added to and took away from the Torah and ultimately disobeyed the Torah through their laws and traditions. They were doing what they wanted to do and not what He commanded to do. Yahushua compared them to *"whitewashed tombs which indeed appear beautiful outwardly, but inside are full of dead men's bones and all uncleanness."* Matthew 23:27

They were declared hypocrites because they professed to be obedient teachers, but they were lawless. This is the same condition that many Christian teachers find themselves today. There are many well-meaning preachers and teachers who are simply repeating the lies and traditions they have been taught. They are leading the sheep away from the Tree of Life to the broad way that leads *many* to destruction.[103]

If you desire to obey and diligently press in with all your heart, there will be mercy and forgiveness when you stumble and fall. That provision was always in the Covenant promise.

On the other hand, if you reject the Commandments and choose to live in lawlessness, then your fate is sealed. Even though provision was made by the Messiah through His shed blood, your actions result in a refusal to enter through the door to the Kingdom.

Again, the poignant passage from the Book of

---

[102] This is one of the distinctions Paul attempted to make in his various letters. There were those who claimed that circumcision in the flesh was a prerequisite to salvation. He called them "The Circumcision" and stressed that it was a matter of the heart not of the flesh. (Colossians 2:11). It is important to remember that Abram first entered into Covenant with YHWH while he was uncircumcised. The circumcision of the flesh came after his demonstration of belief exercised when he left Babylon.

[103] Matthew 7:13

Hebrews is worth repeating: "*[26] For if we sin willfully after we have received the knowledge of the truth, there no longer remains a sacrifice for sins, [27] but a certain fearful expectation of judgment, and fiery indignation which will devour the adversaries. [28] Anyone who has rejected Moses' law (the Torah) dies without mercy on the testimony of two or three witnesses. [29] Of how much worse punishment, do you suppose, will he be thought worthy who has trampled the Son of Elohim underfoot, counted the blood of the Covenant by which he was sanctified a common thing, and insulted the Spirit of grace? [30] For we know Him who said, 'Vengeance is Mine, I will repay,'"says YHWH. And again, 'YHWH will judge His people.' [31] It is a fearful thing to fall into the hands of the living Elohim.*" Hebrews 10:26-31

That is the point of the Passover. The Blood of the Lamb was placed on the doorposts of those who were circumcised – those who obeyed the Commandments and were in the Covenant.

Notice that the text refers to the "knowledge of the truth" and we are not supposed to sin after receiving that knowledge. This ties in with the prophecy given by Hosea.

> "My people are destroyed for lack of knowledge.
> Because you have rejected knowledge,
> I also will reject you from being priest for Me;
> Because you have forgotten the Torah of your Elohim,
> I also will forget your children."
> Hosea 4:6

Whenever Elohim refers to "My people" He is talking about those who are in Covenant with Him, namely Yisrael. Remember that Yisrael was supposed to be a nation of priests through obedience to the Torah. As they lived out the Torah, they were supposed to teach the Torah to the Nations.[104] This never changed.

---

[104] "And you shall be to Me a kingdom of priests and a holy nation.' These are the words which you shall speak to the children of Yisrael." Exodus 19:6

Peter, in one of his letters included in the New Testament wrote: "*⁵ you also, as living stones, are being built up a spiritual house, a holy priesthood, to offer up spiritual sacrifices acceptable to Elohim through Yahushua Messiah . . . ⁷ Therefore, to you who believe, He is precious; but to those who are disobedient, 'The stone which the builders rejected has become the chief cornerstone, ⁸ and 'A stone of stumbling and a rock of offense.' They stumble, being disobedient to the word, to which they also were appointed. ⁹ But you are a chosen generation, a royal priesthood, a holy (set apart) nation, His own special people, that you may proclaim the praises of Him who called you out of darkness into His marvelous light; ¹⁰ who once were not a people but are now the people of Elohim, who had not obtained mercy but now have obtained mercy.*" 1 Peter 2:5, 7-10

See how those who believe are juxtaposed against those who are disobedient to the Word. Those who believe are those who obey the Word. Again, those who obey the Word are "*a royal priesthood and a holy nation*". This is clearly Yisrael.

In fact, in his letter Peter is specifically referring to the promises concerning the restoration of the house of Yisrael as prophesied by Hosea. The house of Yisrael was declared "not My people" by YHWH after they had broken the Covenant; He divorced them, but there was an assurance that they would once again be the people of Elohim.[105]

Peter even prefaced his letter by explicitly stating that he was writing to the "*elect according to the foreknowledge of Elohim the Father, in sanctification of the Spirit, for obedience and sprinkling of the blood of Yahushua Messiah*" 1 Peter 1:2. He was referring to those "*who are kept by the power of Elohim through faith for salvation ready to be revealed in the last time.*" 1 Peter 1:5

The "sprinkling of the blood" of the Messiah is reminiscent of when Yisrael was sprinkled with blood at Sinai as they entered into a marriage Covenant with

---

[105] See Hosea 1:1-11

- 76 -

YHWH.[106] Peter is referring to the Renewed Covenant that the Messiah established with the house of Yisrael by the shedding and sprinkling of His blood.

It is important to note that they are being kept for salvation at *"the last time"*, better known as *"the end of days"* or *"the end of the age."* It is clear from Peter that salvation will occur at the end.

YHWH will truly save His people, but His people are only those who follow Him and walk in His Covenant. It will not involve going to heaven and floating on the clouds. Rather, that salvation will be for those who have prepared themselves to be priests of the Most High. They will be permitted back into Eden to serve in the Kingdom of YHWH ruled by Messiah on this planet.

If you believe that the Messiah died for your sins so that you can keep on sinning, then you do not understand the Creator nor His Covenant Plan of redemption. You have been taught a lie and if you continue to live and believe that lie you will not enter into the Kingdom.

This truth is clearly provided in the Scriptures. *"Whoever abides in Him does not sin. Whoever sins has neither seen Him nor known Him."* 1 John 3:6. If you continue to sin then you are lawless. The Messiah will reject you because He does not know you due to your lawlessness.

You will not be in the Kingdom, nor will you be part of the house, represented by the New Jerusalem. *"But outside are dogs and sorcerers and sexually immoral and murderers and idolaters, and whoever loves and practices a lie."* Revelation 22:15. Notice that the people outside the New Jerusalem are defined by their lawless deeds.

There is a deceiver who has been lying to mankind since the Garden. He may be able to kill your flesh, but he cannot kill your soul – you alone are responsible for your

---

[106] *"And Moses took the blood, sprinkled it on the people, and said, 'This is the blood of the covenant which YHWH has made with you according to all these words.'"* Exodus 24:8.

soul.

If he can get you to willfully disobey the Commandments of Elohim, then you will fall under judgment – sometimes referred to as being *"under law"* (Romans 6:14-15) or subject to *"the law of sin and death"*. (Romans 8:2)

This was how Balaam got Yisrael to fall under a curse. He was a prophet for hire who was not permitted to directly curse Yisrael on behalf of Balak, sovereign of Moab, along with the elders of Midian. Instead, he instructed them to entice Yisrael into adultery so that they would be cursed by YHWH.[107]

This is the same tactic and method used by satan. If he can get us to live a life of lawlessness then he has succeeded in his quest to destroy us. He doesn't have to kill us. All he has to do is get us to live lawless lives and we essentially bring about our own destruction.

When we willfully disobey the Commandments we are subject to separation from Elohim, which leads to death. This started in the Garden and mankind has been under that death penalty until Messiah, through grace, delivered us from the death sentence provided in the Torah. Both the penalty and the solution were provided through the Torah.

The serpent deceived the woman and enticed her to break the Commandment not to eat of a certain tree. It was such a simple Command, certainly not too difficult. But she was enticed and told that Elohim was a liar. She believed the serpent and both the woman and the man brought about their own destruction. If we believe the same lie then we too will be cast out and punished for our lawless deeds.[108]

Peter warned of those who fell into this trap in one of his letters:

---

[107] See Numbers Chapter 22 to 24. See also Numbers 31:16.

[108] Thankfully, YHWH revealed that He was willing to atone (cover) our sins by the shedding of blood. This picture was presented to us when He covered the man and the woman with the skins of the sacrificial offering.

"[12] But these, like natural brute beasts made to be caught and destroyed, speak evil of the things they do not understand, and will utterly perish in their own corruption, [13] and will receive the wages of unrighteousness, as those who count it pleasure to carouse in the daytime. They are spots and blemishes, carousing in their own deceptions while they feast with you, [14] having eyes full of adultery and that cannot cease from sin, enticing unstable souls. They have a heart trained in covetous practices, and are accursed children. [15] They have forsaken the right way and gone astray, following the way of Balaam the son of Beor, who loved the wages of unrighteousness; [16] but he was rebuked for his iniquity: a dumb donkey speaking with a man's voice restrained the madness of the prophet. [17] These are wells without water, clouds carried by a tempest, for whom is reserved the blackness of darkness forever. [18] For when they speak great swelling words of emptiness, they allure through the lusts of the flesh, through lewdness, the ones who have actually escaped from those who live in error. [19] While they promise them liberty, they themselves are slaves of corruption; for by whom a person is overcome, by him also he is brought into bondage. [20] For if, after they have escaped the pollutions of the world through the knowledge of the Master and Savior Messiah Yahushua, they are again entangled in them and overcome, the latter end is worse for them than the beginning. [21] For it would have been better for them not to have known the way of righteousness, than having known it, to turn from the holy Commandment delivered to them. [22] But it has happened to them according to the true proverb: 'A dog returns to his own vomit,' and, 'a sow, having washed, to her wallowing in the mire.'" 2 Peter 2:12-22

So, we see that those who go the way of Balaam and return to their lawless ways after receiving forgiveness are likened to dogs returning to their own vomit. They have a certain expectation of judgment awaiting them.

The way of righteousness involves following the Commandments. It is the way that leads to salvation. I hear many Christians declare their "liberty" as if that means they are free to disobey the Commandments. That is a lie straight from the serpent in the Garden.

When we place our faith in the work of the Messiah we are free from the curse of sin and death by His atoning blood. We are free from the bondage of sin and we can then walk in the blessings of the Torah. That is the liberty that we need to desire and claim.[109]

Yahushua also warned the Assembly at Pergamos about this specific deception used by Balaam: *"[14] But I have a few things against you, because you have there those who hold the doctrine of Balaam, who taught Balak to put a stumbling block before the children of Yisrael, to eat things sacrificed to idols, and to commit sexual immorality. [15] Thus you also have those who hold the doctrine of the Nicolaitans, which thing I hate. [16] Repent, or else I will come to you quickly and will fight against them with the sword of My mouth."* Revelation 2:14-16. Again, the stumbling block is the lie that leads people to disobey the Commandments. This results in them being judged and punished.

At the end of the age, Elohim will judge the living and the dead. Here is a vivid picture of that final judgment: *"[12] And I saw the dead, small and great, standing before Elohim, and books were opened. And another book was opened, which is the Book of Life. And the dead were judged according to their works, by the things which were written in the books. [13] The sea gave up the dead who were in it, and Death and Hades delivered up the dead who were in them. And they were judged, each one according to his works."* Revelation 20:12-13. The dead are judged by their works, not by their internal decisions or confessions of faith.

Yahushua actually revealed how He would conduct His judgment.

---

[109] James 1:25

"*³¹ When the Son of Man comes in His glory, and all the holy angels with Him, then He will sit on the throne of His glory. ³² All the nations will be gathered before Him, and He will separate them one from another, as a shepherd divides his sheep from the goats. ³³ And He will set the sheep on His right hand, but the goats on the left. ³⁴ Then the King will say to those on His right hand, 'Come, you blessed of My Father, inherit the kingdom prepared for you from the foundation of the world: ³⁵ for I was hungry and you gave Me food; I was thirsty and you gave Me drink; I was a stranger and you took Me in; ³⁶ I was naked and you clothed Me; I was sick and you visited Me; I was in prison and you came to Me.' ³⁷ Then the righteous will answer Him, saying, 'Master, when did we see You hungry and feed You, or thirsty and give You drink? ³⁸ When did we see You a stranger and take You in, or naked and clothe You? ³⁹ Or when did we see You sick, or in prison, and come to You?' ⁴⁰ And the King will answer and say to them, 'Assuredly, I say to you, inasmuch as you did it to one of the least of these My brethren, you did it to Me.' ⁴¹ Then He will also say to those on the left hand, 'Depart from Me, you cursed, into the everlasting fire prepared for the devil and his angels: ⁴² for I was hungry and you gave Me no food; I was thirsty and you gave Me no drink; ⁴³ I was a stranger and you did not take Me in, naked and you did not clothe Me, sick and in prison and you did not visit Me. ⁴⁴ Then they also will answer Him, saying, 'Master, when did we see You hungry or thirsty or a stranger or naked or sick or in prison, and did not minister to You?' ⁴⁵ Then He will answer them, saying, 'Assuredly, I say to you, inasmuch as you did not do it to one of the least of these, you did not do it to Me.' ⁴⁶ And these will go away into everlasting punishment, but the righteous into eternal life.'" Matthew 25:31-46*

Imagine that! This great judgment is focused on works. Notice the sheep are referred to as "righteous." They are defined by their actions, because the righteous instructions are found in the Torah. The Messiah will will save His righteous sheep. They are the ones who have remained faithful and proven to be trustworthy. They are the overcomers and their names will be confessed before the Father. Their names will be found in the Book of Life. They will not be blotted out.[110]

Your name must be found written in the Book of Life, also known as the Book of the Living. It contains the names of the righteous. All of the wicked are blotted out of the Book of the Living.[111]

I cannot count the people that I have heard throughout my life declaring that they are a "good person." Based upon their definition of "good," they believe that they are ready to stand before the Great Judge. The problem is that Yahushua said: *"No one is good but One, that is, Elohim. But if you want to enter into life, keep the Commandments."* Matthew 19:17[112]

It is not our definition of good that gets us into the Kingdom. Rather, it is the Commandments that lead us into the Kingdom once cleansed by the Blood of the Lamb. This is the point when Elohim steps in and saves His people from the fate that they once deserved. If you have disobeyed the Commandments you deserve the appropriate punishment "under the law," unless you rely upon the atoning sacrifice provided through the Torah.

The entire purpose of the work of the Messiah was to

---

[110] See Revelation 2:1 to 3:22 and specifically Revelation 3:5.
[111] See Psalm 69:28. This would appear to fly in the face of the popular doctrine known as "eternal security". Clearly a person's name can be blotted out of the Book of the Living. The Messiah was very clear that He would not blot out the names of those who overcome.
[112] See also Mark 10:18 and Luke 18:19

make it possible for us to enter into the Kingdom of YHWH. That is why He instructed His disciples to go make disciples of all the nations, *"teaching them to observe all things that I have commanded you."*[113] This was known as the Great Commission and it was the commission of the Kingdom of Yisrael.

Yisrael had failed in their commission to be priests. They broke the Covenant, they were divided and they were exiled to the four corners of the planet. Yahushua came and died to pay the penalty for Yisrael breaking the Covenant. By His life, death and resurrection, Yisrael could be regathered and restored. Through this regathering, the nations would also be drawn into the Kingdom. This was the Good News of the Kingdom. Every kingdom has rules and the Torah contains the rules of the Kingdom of YHWH.

If you believe in the Messiah and truly love Him, then you will do as He says so that you can dwell with Him in the Kingdom. He clearly said: *"If you love Me, keep My Commandments."* John 14:15. Your obedience is your expression of love and it is the way to salvation. We are all participants in the salvation process.

Ultimately, salvation is not a decision that you alone make. It is all up to the One Who provides salvation. It is a gift given to those who obey Him. Only the blood of the Messiah can cleanse and atone for our sins. It is then our obedience that keeps us clean.

This is a process and the reason why we continue to rehearse the Feasts of YHWH each and every year as they teach us the Covenant path that leads to salvation. The life, death and resurrection of the Messiah was centered on fulfilling those Appointed Times[114] and, through His

---

[113] Matthew 28:18

[114] The Appointed Times are specific "appointments" that are scheduled each year by YHWH. They are known as "moadim" in Hebrew, and they are specifically designed for those in Covenant with Him. They are often mistakenly referred to as "Jewish Holidays" but that is an error. YHWH specifically states that they are His Appointed Times. (see

fulfillment, we see the clear path to salvation.

If you made a decision to believe in the Messiah, then you must act on that decision. If you truly have faith in the work of the Messiah, then you will do as He said and follow Him. The question is not whether you are presently saved, that will occur in the end.

The question to ask is whether or not you are in a covenant relationship so that your sins may be atoned by the sprinkling of the blood of the Lamb.

Your obedience to the terms of the Covenant will demonstrate whether you are in that Covenant relationship or not. If you are in the Covenant, renewed by the Messiah, then you are known by Him. He will wash you clean so that death will pass over you and your household. He will count you as one of His, He will redeem you and fill you with the Spirit so that you have the Torah on your mind and in your heart.

This is the Covenant path that Messiah blazed and fulfilled through the Appointed Times, and this is the way that leads us to salvation.

Modern Christianity has tried to make this path easy – the Messiah said it was not! He warned that "... *narrow is the gate and difficult is the way which leads to life, and there are few who find it.*" Matthew 7:14

You must determine where your salvation comes from and then walk in that way. You must chose obedience or lawlessness – life or death. Choose life![115]

Leviticus 23:1). Therefore they are times to be observed by all who are in Covenant with Him. For a more detailed discussion of the Appointed Times see the Walk in the Light series book entitled *Appointed Times*.

[115] Deuteronomy 30:19

The Walk in the Light Series

living.

Book 10   Appointed Times – Discusses the appointed times established by the Creator, often erroneously considered to be "Jewish" holidays, and their critical importance to the understanding of prophetic fulfillment of the Scriptural promises.

Book 11   Pagan Holidays – Discusses the pagan origins of some popular Christian holidays which have replaced the Appointed Times.

Book 12   The Final Shofar – Examines the ancient history of the earth and prepares the Believer for the deceptions coming in the end of the age. It also discusses the walk required by the Scriptures to be an overcomer and to endure to the end.

To order any of the books in the Walk in the Light Series in print or e-book format visit:

www.shemayisrael.net

The Shema
Deuteronomy 6:4-5

Traditional English Translation

Hear, O Israel: The LORD our God, the LORD is one!
You shall love the LORD your God with all your heart,
with all your soul, and with all your strength.

Corrected English Translation

Hear, O Yisrael: YHWH our Elohim, YHWH is one
(unified)!
You shall love YHWH your Elohim with all your heart,
with all your soul, and with all your strength.

Modern Hebrew Text

שְׁמַ֫ע יִשְׂרָאֵל֫ יהוה אלהינו יהוה אחד֫
ואהבת את יהוה אלהיך בכל-לבבך ובכל-נפשך ובכל מאדך

Ancient Hebrew Text

◁ꓧꓘ ꓯＹꓯƖ Ｙꓱꓛꓘ ꓯＹꓯɩ ꓘꓱꓯWɩ ⊙ꓯW
ꓱꓯꓖ-ꓛＹꓖ ꓱꓱꓘꓘ ꓯＹꓯɩ ꓫꓘ ꓫꓖꓯꓘＹ
ꓱ◁ꓘꓯ-ꓛＹꓖＹ ꓱW ꓕꓯ-ꓛＹꓖＹ

Hebrew Text Transliterated

Shema, Yisra'el: YHWH Elohenu, YHWH echad!
V-ahavta et YHWH Elohecha b-chol l'bacha ub-chol
naf'sh'cha ub-chol m'odecha.

The Shema has traditionally been one of the most important prayers in
Judaism and was declared the first (resheet) of all the Commandments by
The Messiah. (Mark 12:29-30)

Made in the USA
San Bernardino, CA
05 November 2015